AF617925

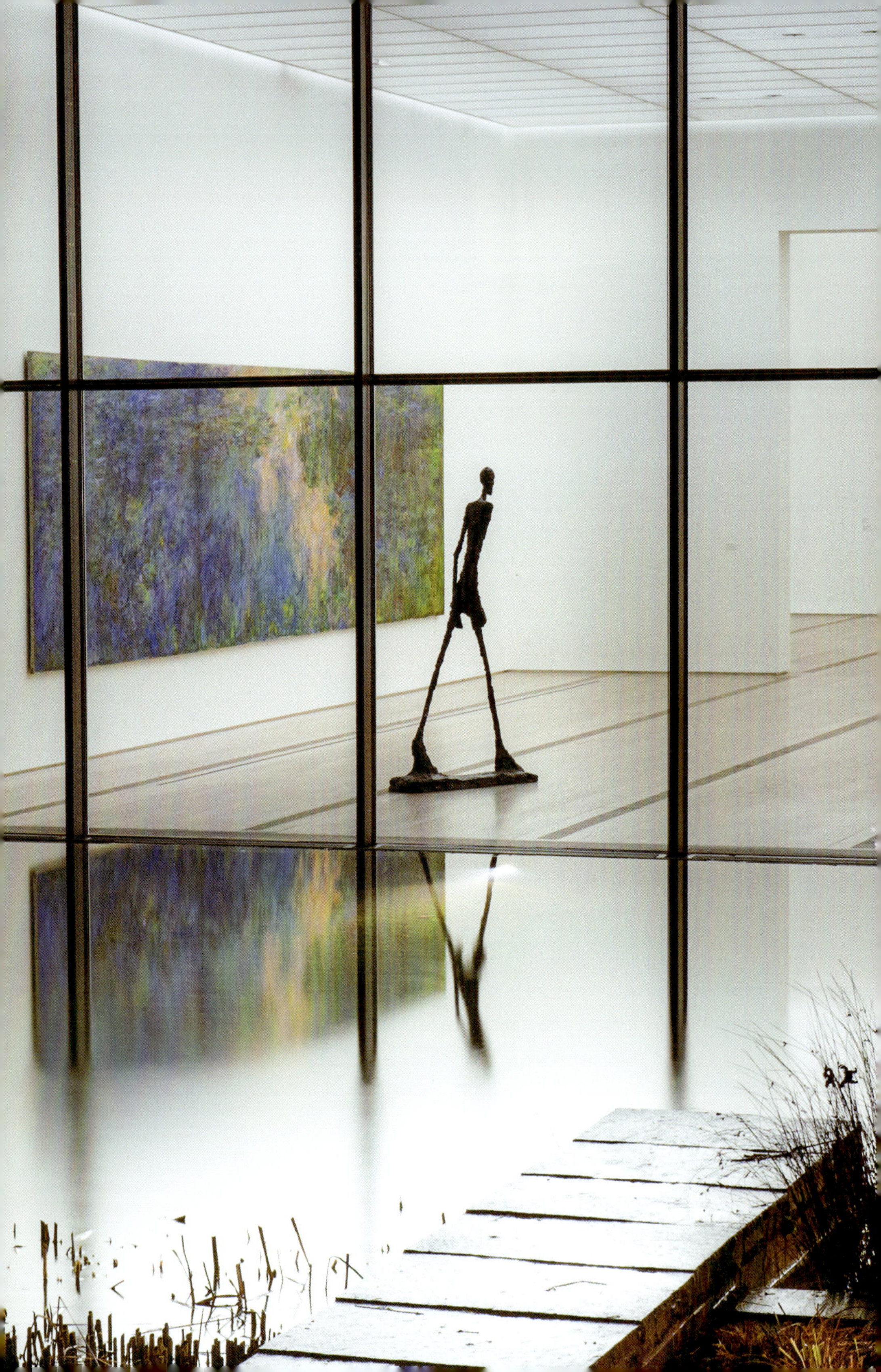

Fondation Beyeler 25 Highlights

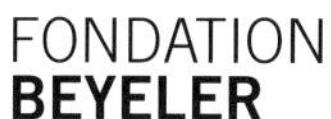

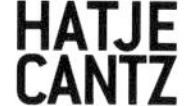

The Collection of the Fondation Beyeler

The Beyeler Collection forms the nucleus of the Fondation Beyeler and marks its thematic starting point. Over a period of more than fifty years, Ernst Beyeler and his wife, Hildy, assembled a collection of outstanding examples of modern art, parallel to their activities as successful gallery owners. The collection, mainly comprising paintings and sculptures, was made accessible to the public by establishing it as a foundation. In 1997, Ernst and Hildy Beyeler opened the Fondation Beyeler in the much-praised museum building designed by Renzo Piano in Ernst Beyeler's hometown of Riehen, near Basel. The museum and its park setting combine art, nature, and architecture to create a unique sensory appeal.

The exquisite Beyeler Collection begins with masterpieces of late nineteenth-century avant-garde art, including paintings by the Impressionists Claude Monet and Edgar Degas, and the Post-Impressionists Paul Cézanne, Vincent van Gogh, and Henri Rousseau. The collection's focus is on classical modern art, encompassing the various progressive tendencies in Western art from around 1900 to 1940. This includes pioneering European artists such as Henri Matisse, Joan Miró, Max Ernst, Paul Klee, Wassily Kandinsky, Constantin Brancusi, and Piet Mondrian, with substantial groups of works or, in some cases, single works that have an outstanding exemplary significance. The museum's largest single holding of works by a modern artist is that of Pablo Picasso, comprising over thirty major paintings, sculptures, and works on paper from nearly every phase of the artist's oeuvre. While the art of the postwar period is represented by impressive groups of works by formative European artists such as Alberto Giacometti, Jean Dubuffet, and Francis Bacon, the Beyeler Collection also reveals a growing interest in US-American art of that time, notably in Abstract Expressionism and Pop Art, with seminal figures such as Jackson Pollock, Barnett Newman, Mark Rothko, Andy Warhol, and Ellsworth Kelly. The next generation is exemplified mainly by the work of German painters, including Anselm Kiefer, Georg Baselitz, and Gerhard Richter. This collection of modern art is complemented by thirty works from Africa, Oceania, and Alaska, objects that Ernst and Hildy Beyeler acquired in view of their significance for the development of modernism.

These holdings of modern art acquired by the museum's founders can now be considered "historic" works of art, and they remain the heart of the museum; since the death of its patrons, however, the Fondation Beyeler has continued to expand the collection primarily in the area of contemporary art. Particular emphasis has been placed on the work of women artists, who were previously underrepresented in the collection. Painting and sculpture remain at the forefront, with the acquisition of groups of works by notable artists such as Louise Bourgeois, Marlene Dumas, Roni Horn, Rachel Whiteread, and Thomas Schütte; the focus has also been widened to include photography and new media, along with film and installation art.

Among the acquisitions in this area are an extensive ensemble of photographs by Wolfgang Tillmans and installations incorporating light, film, and sound by Felix Gonzalez-Torres, Philippe Parreno, and Susan Philipsz. With these more recent accessions, the collection of the Fondation Beyeler now consists of some four hundred works of modern and contemporary art.

This publication presents twenty-five exemplary works from the collection with illustrations and short commentaries. The texts offer an accessible introduction to the works, commenting on their particular artistic significance and providing insights into the profile of the collection and its history. With masterpieces of Post-Impressionism, classical modern art, and the postwar movements up to the present, the selection of works reflects the variety and range of the collection of an open and vibrant museum that promotes access to art and cultural education as well as aesthetic and sensory experiences and opportunities for interpersonal encounter and exchange.

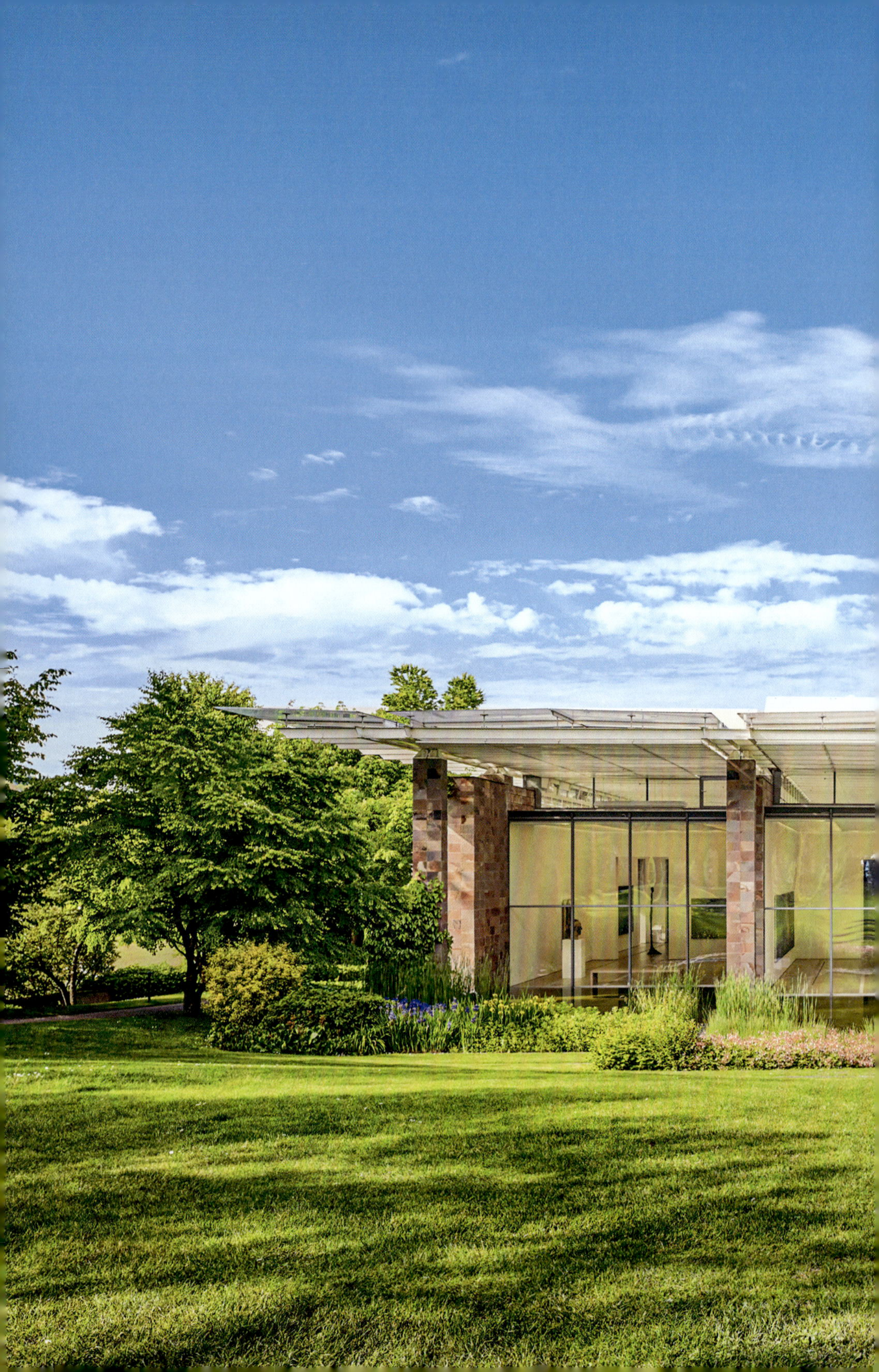

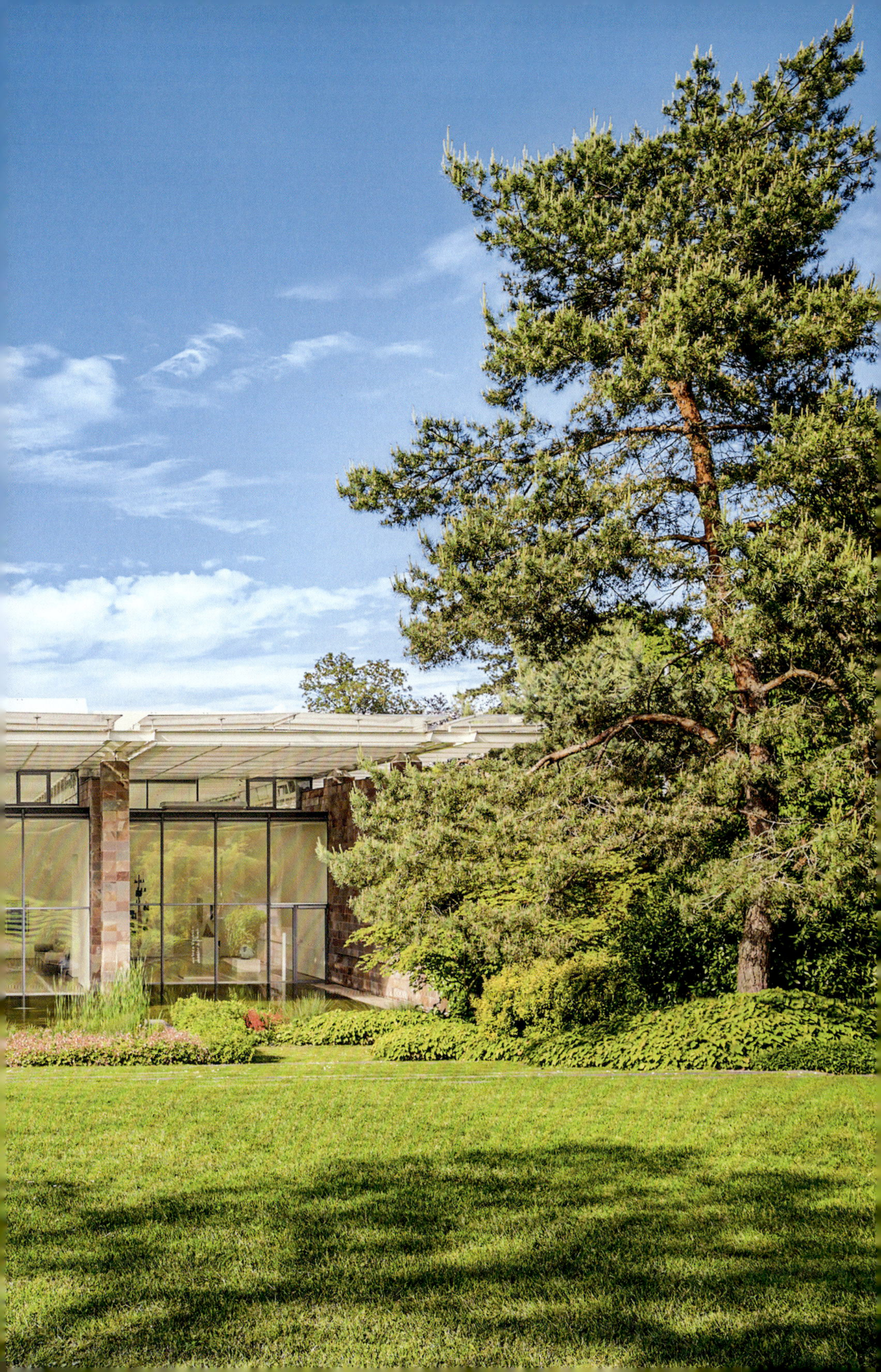

Paul Cézanne (1839–1906)

Madame Cézanne à la chaise jaune

Madame Cézanne in a Yellow Chair, 1888–90

Oil on canvas, 80.3 × 64.3 cm

Paul Cézanne, celebrated as a pioneer of modern art, is represented in the museum collection with no less than seven works in various genres, including landscapes and still lifes in oil and watercolor, in addition to this portrait of his wife.

Madame Cézanne à la chaise jaune shows Hortense Fiquet (1850–1922), who had been married to the artist since 1886, in the couple's Paris apartment. Cézanne painted nearly thirty pictures of Hortense. They were the result of a long-standing cooperation between the artist and his wife, despite the notoriously complicated nature of their relationship, and are among his most innovative portraits. Of the four versions of Hortense seated on a chair and wearing a red dress, the portrait in the Beyeler Collection is the most personal, showing particularly close eye contact between artist and model. Hortense's facial expression, however, is as difficult to read as the space surrounding her since Cézanne dispenses with linear perspective and the coherent rendering of spatial depth—as exemplified by the broken line of the dado rail in the background. Instead, his approach is based on constructing the picture from geometric areas of color, which rely entirely on juxtaposition for plastic effect.

Besides challenging traditional conceptions of space, the picture also has an immediacy that contributes to its undisputed quality. In particular, the treatment of the model's folded hands and lap—interspersing the color with patches of blank canvas—brilliantly exemplifies Cézanne's progressive conception of the picture, playfully experimenting with the idea of the unfinished work.

The enduring influence of Cézanne's groundbreaking oeuvre is apparent in pictures by many of his successors, such as in Pablo Picasso's *Femme en vert (Dora)* (1944), also in the collection. Picasso hugely admired Cézanne, whom he is said to have described as "the father of us all."

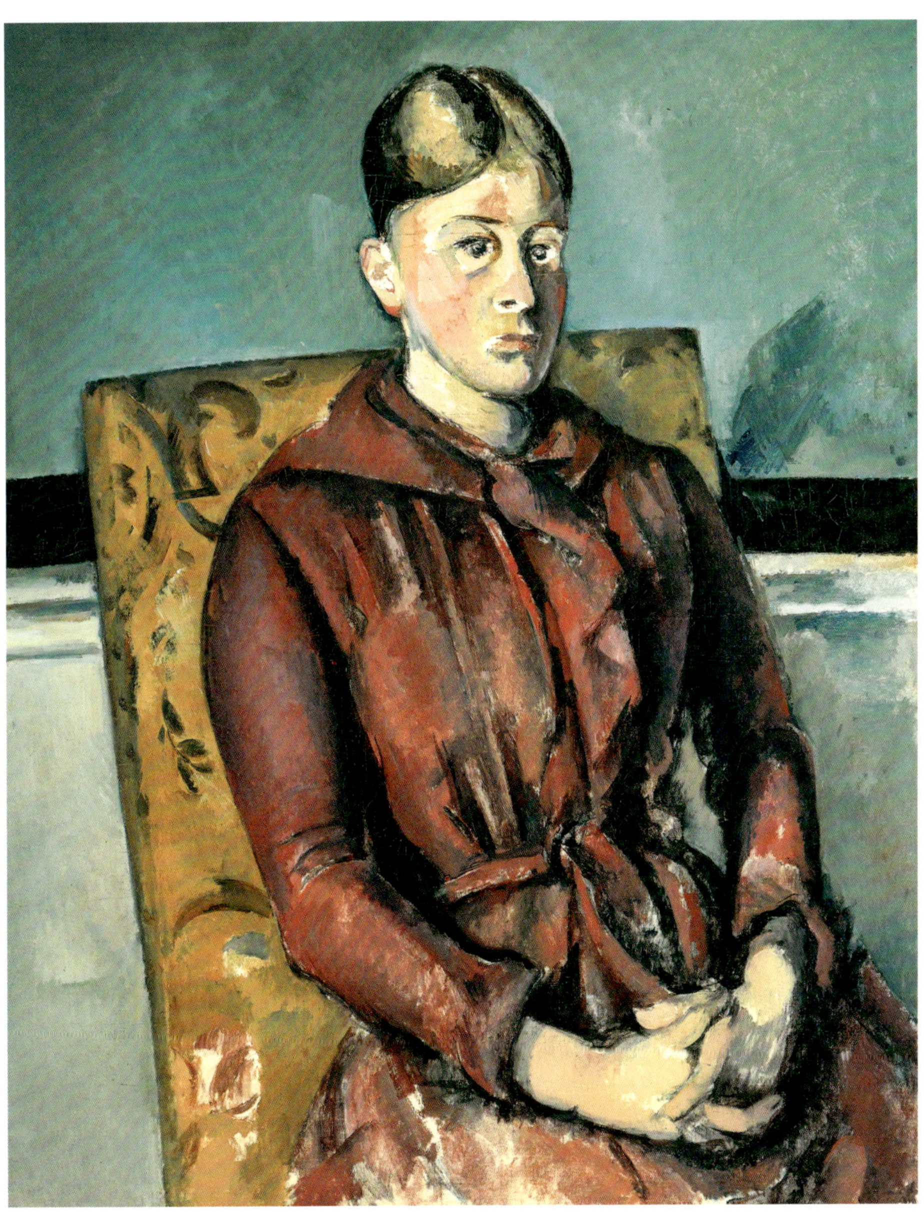

Claude Monet (1840–1926)

Le bassin aux nymphéas

Water Lily Pond, ca. 1917–20

Oil on canvas, triptych, each panel 200.7 × 301 cm

In 1883 Claude Monet rented a sizeable farmhouse for himself and his large family in the village of Giverny, west of Paris. He transformed the orchard on the property into a garden with flower beds, which provided inspiration for his pictures. In 1890 he purchased the house, and three years later bought an adjacent plot of land, where he laid out a water garden with a Japanese footbridge inspired by Japanese woodcuts. Up to the time of his death, in 1926, this ensemble was his preferred source of motifs, and from 1914 onward, he painted practically only pictures based on the garden. For a painter to design a park purely in order to supply himself with ideas must surely be unique in the history of art.
The celebrated water lily triptych in the Beyeler Collection is connected with an overarching project that occupied Monet from around 1917 until his death; it became a monument marking the end of World War I, which the artist donated to the French state. The work is displayed in the Orangerie in the Jardin des Tuileries in Paris, as a counter-image to war and a place of memory for nature in the city.

Along the way to this goal, Monet created many pictures of water lilies, often in multipart formats. The radical approach of the version in the Fondation Beyeler makes it especially impressive. The viewer sees almost nothing but the reflection of the sky and the plants on the surface of the pond.

The water lilies appear to float, as mere traces, in this reflected image. Monet thus transformed an imitation of an imitation into a free, almost gestural form of painting that nevertheless remains indebted to figuration. It seems, however, as if the artist had opened the door to abstract painting. No wonder that Abstract Expressionists such as Joan Mitchell and Sam Francis were great admirers of Monet's water lily paintings.

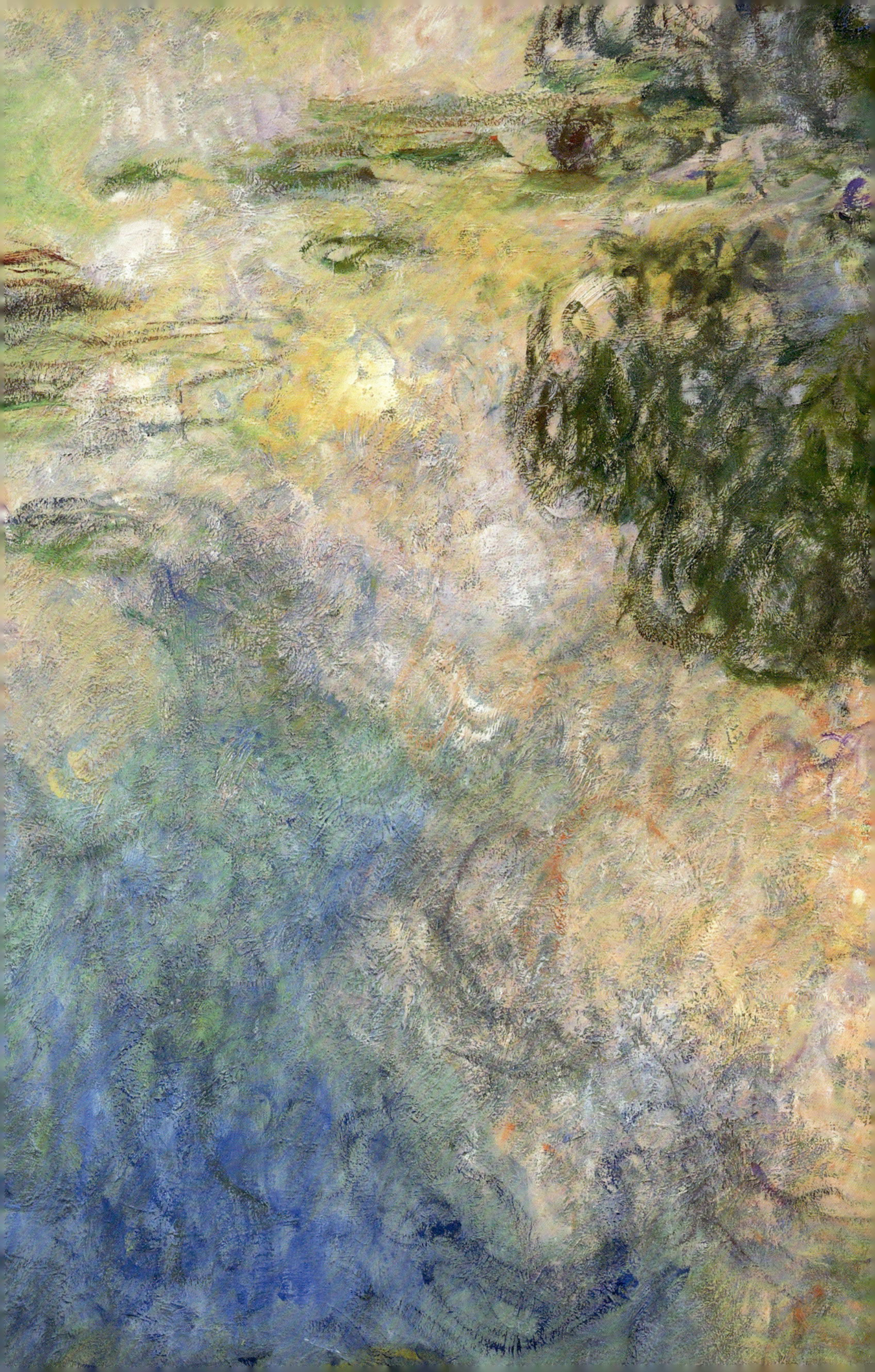

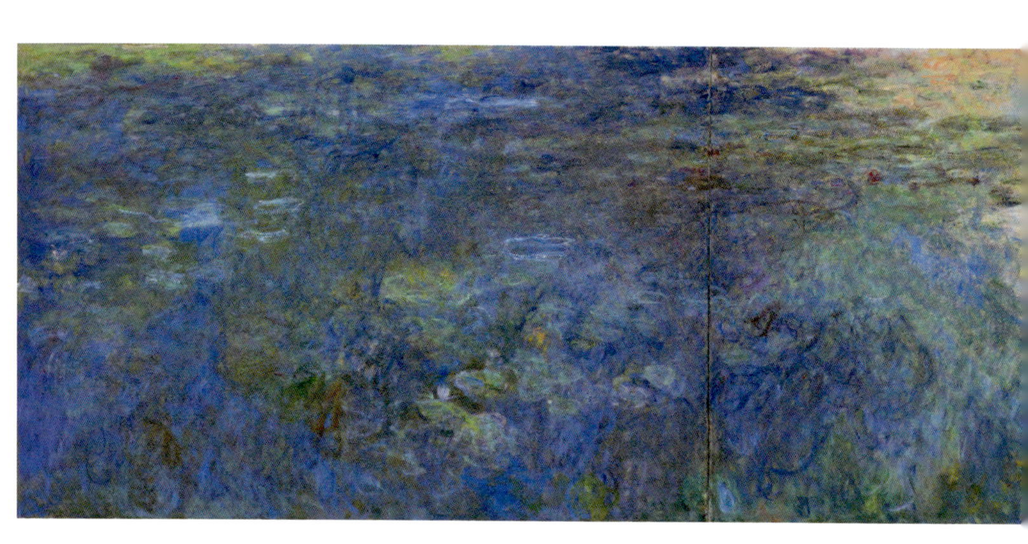

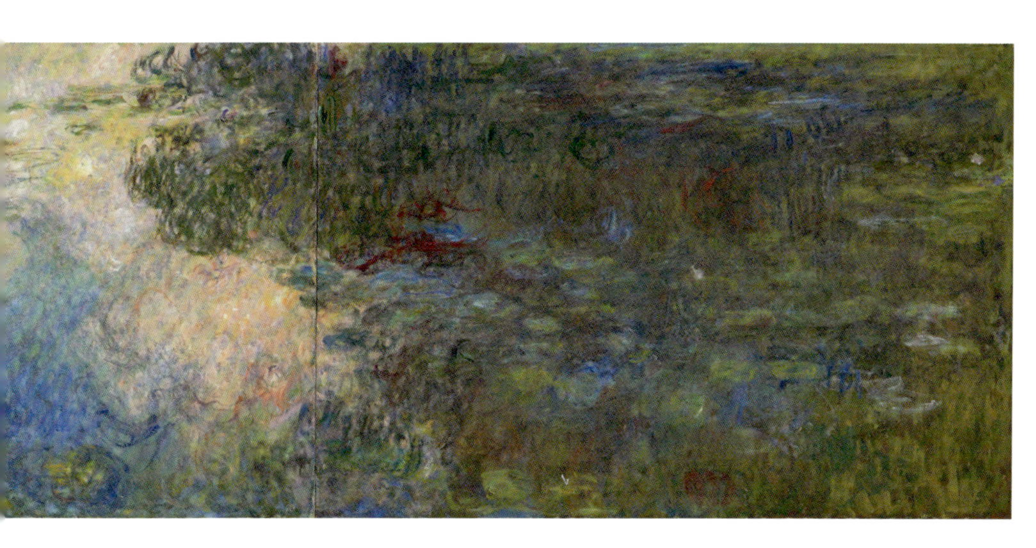

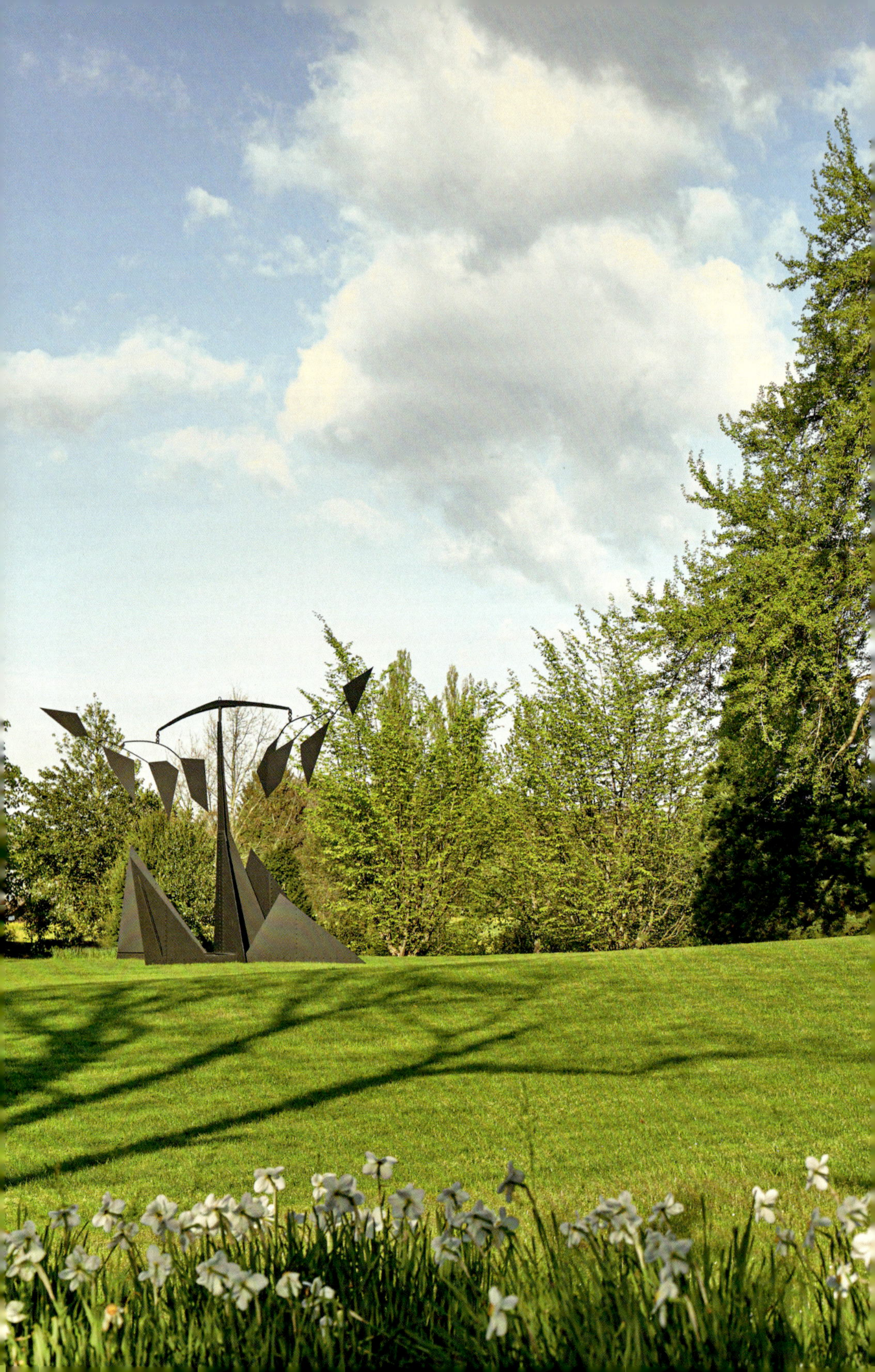

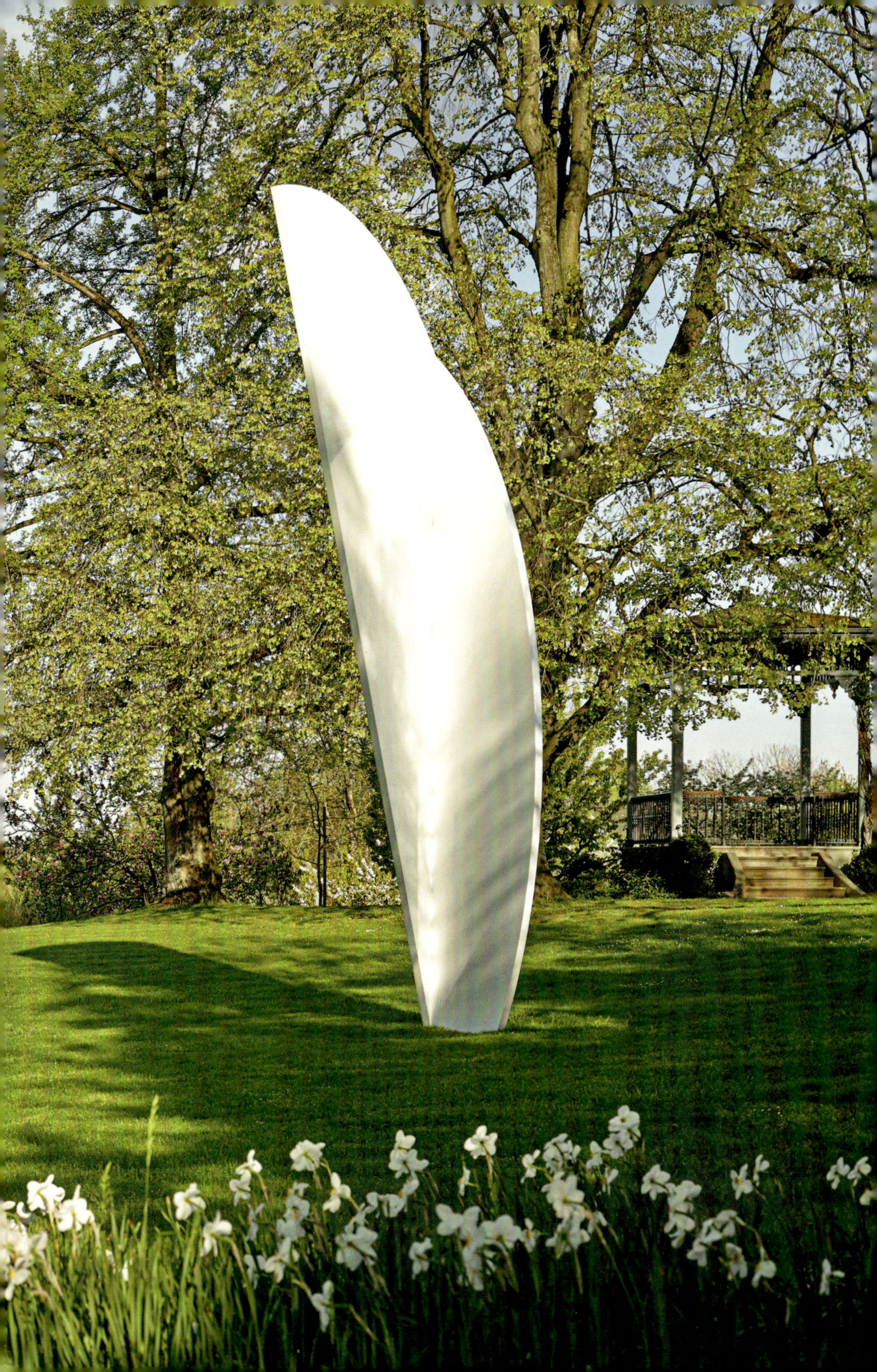

Henri Rousseau (1844–1910)

Le lion, ayant faim, se jette sur l'antilope
The Hungry Lion Attacking an Antelope, 1898/1905
Oil on canvas, 200 × 301 cm

"The lion, being hungry, throws itself on the antelope, [and] devours it;
The panther anxiously awaits the moment when it too can claim its share.
Birds of prey have each torn a piece of flesh from the top of the poor animal,
which sheds a tear. The sun sets."

The full title of this work captures in words a human and emotional view of nature that makes Henri Rousseau's painting truly exceptional. A customs officer who taught himself to paint, Rousseau never set foot outside France, let alone in a jungle. The inspiration for his many jungle pictures came from visits to the botanical gardens of Paris and the world's fair exhibitions in the city at the turn of the century. The central group of figures in the picture, with its deliberately staged appearance, is based on an educational diorama featuring a lion and an antelope that Rousseau had seen in the Paris Museum of Natural History. The figures in the painting are framed by thick foliage in myriad shades of green, elaborately layered and staggered, the leaves parted in places to afford a glimpse of further animals. A stark contrast is supplied by the bloody shreds of flesh in the birds' beaks, and by the antelope's wounds, echoed in the color of the sun in the background. There is a distinct pathos in the central scene, with the tears of the weeping antelope and the positively human appearance of the lion's teeth as it bites into the neck of its prey. Clearly, this artful arrangement of elements formulated with delicate precision is a dramatic rendering of a dreamlike story.
The picture occupies a special place in Rousseau's oeuvre. It is the first painting he showed in a judged exhibition: the 1905 Paris Salon d'Automne. Undated, it was probably made some years earlier, in 1898. It was also the first of his works to make it onto the art market. The initial response of critics and the public to Rousseau's visual inventions was one of consternation. Younger artists such as Robert Delaunay and Pablo Picasso, however, paid tribute to this exceptional painter, who exerted a considerable influence on art in the early twentieth century.

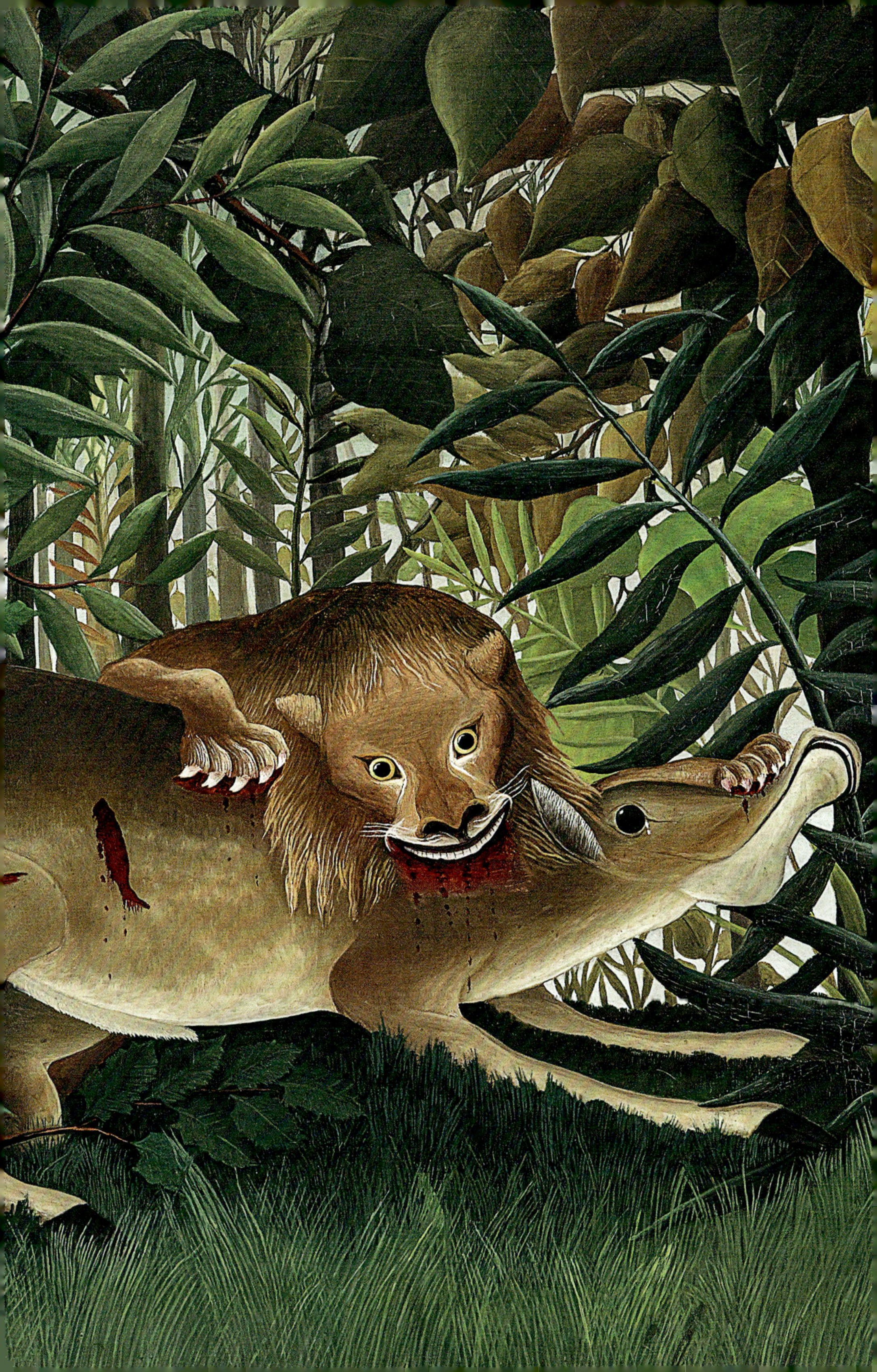

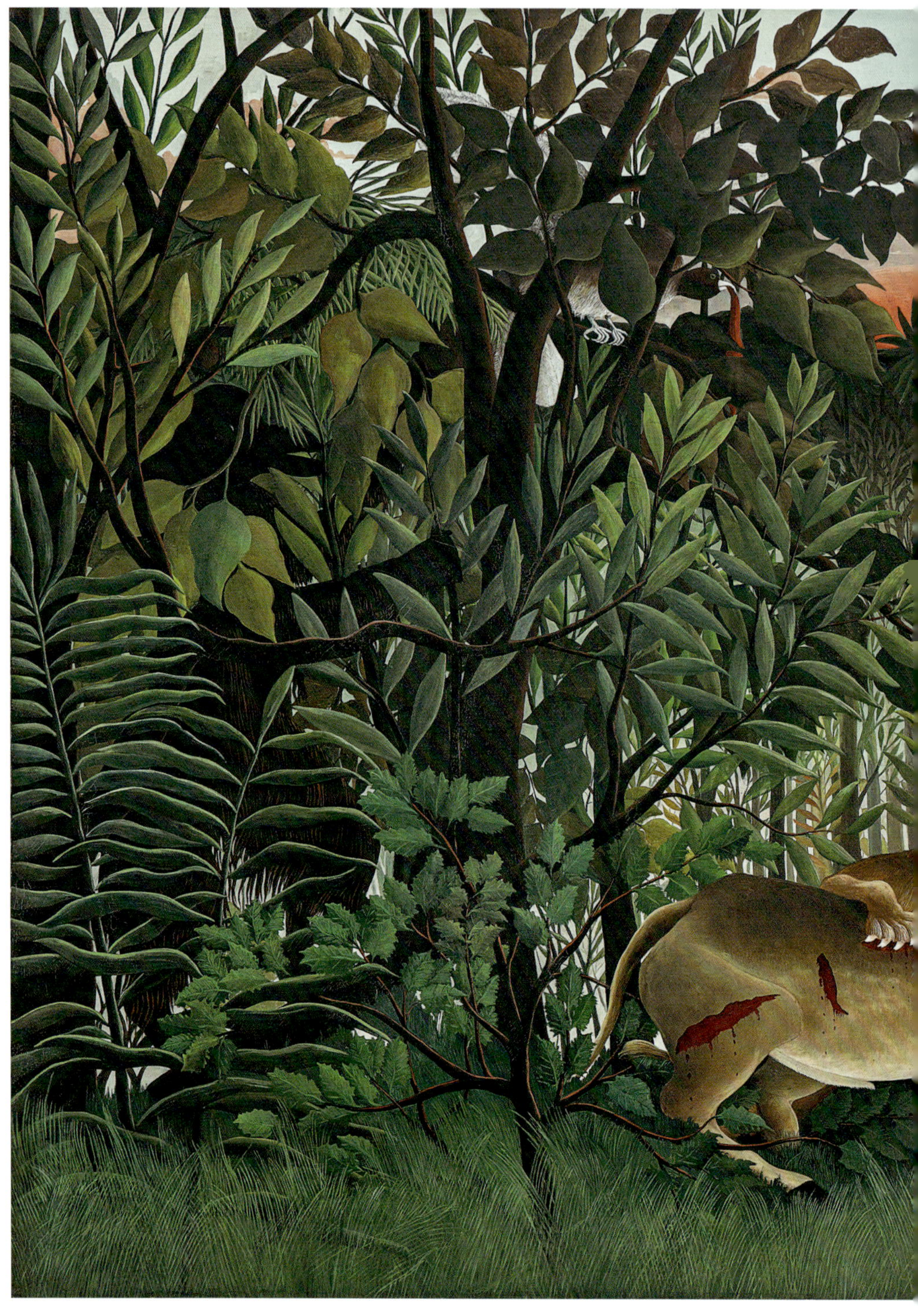

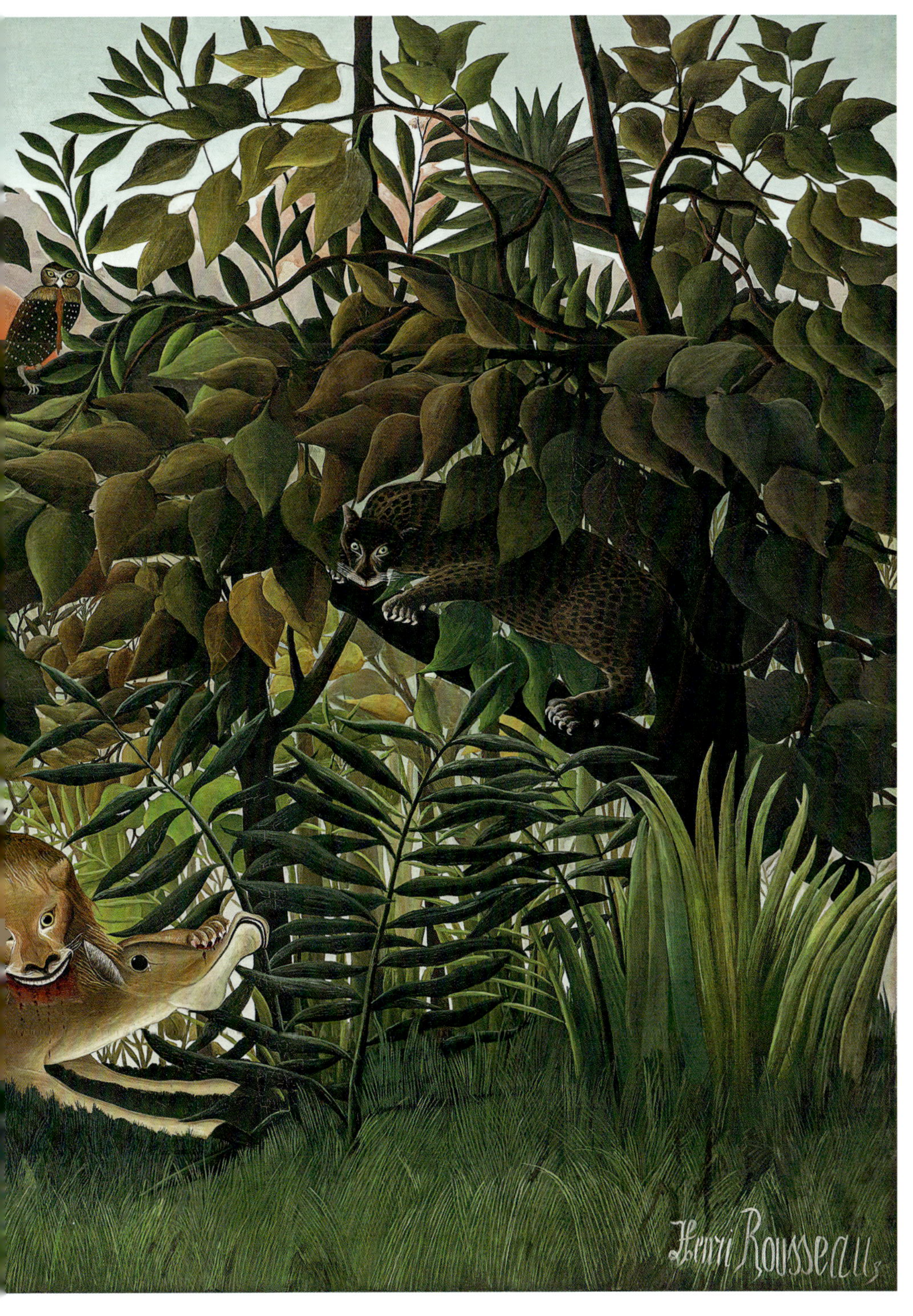
Henri Rousseau

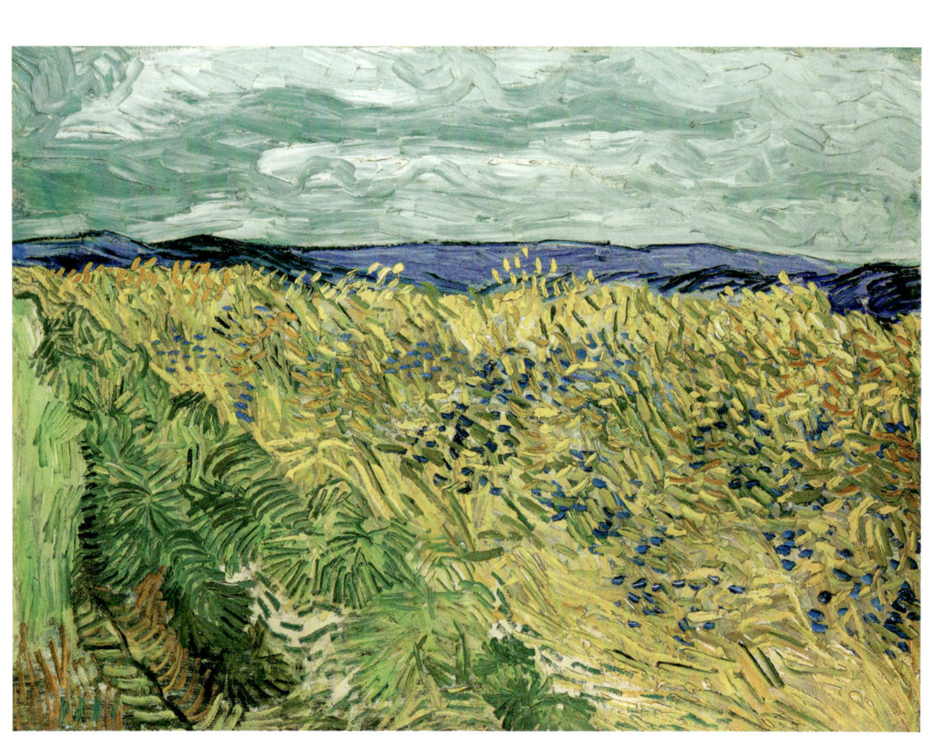

Vincent van Gogh (1853–1890)

Champ de blé aux bleuets

Wheat Field with Cornflowers, 1890

Oil on canvas, 60 × 81 cm

Vincent van Gogh's *Champ de blé aux bleuets* was painted just a few weeks before the artist's death. On May 20, 1890, Van Gogh traveled to Auvers-sur-Oise, a village northwest of Paris, popular with artists, where he lived for the next two months, until his death by suicide. In the countryside he hoped for an improvement in his physical and mental state, and regularly consulted Dr. Paul Gachet, a physician and art collector who was a long-standing supporter of the Impressionists.

The painting marks the beginning of the final, especially productive phase of Van Gogh's work. During the summer months in Auvers he painted over seventy pictures, mostly of the extensive wheat fields in the area. *Champ de blé aux bleuets* also shows a vivid yellow expanse of wheat that could be imagined as continuing endlessly beyond the margins of the canvas. Single cornflowers stand out among the ears of corn, in luminous shades of blue that correspond with the color of the hills on the horizon. A narrow path, visible at the left edge of the canvas, leads deep into the field. An infinite sky, animated by gray-green clouds, looms above the scene. The motif of the wheat field agitated by the wind already seems to reflect the artist's inner turmoil. The swirling brushstrokes, too, with the turbulence that typifies Van Gogh, convey an impression of extreme despair, but also of tremendous creative energy. The paint is applied thickly, in long, sweeping movements, creating a richly structured picture surface that endows the scene with drama and expressive force. In a letter to his mother and his sister, Van Gogh emphasized the impact of the Auvers countryside on his painting: "For my part, I'm wholly absorbed in the vast expanse of wheat fields against the hills, large as a sea, delicate yellow, delicate pale green, delicate purple of a ploughed and weeded piece of land. . . . I'm wholly in a mood of almost too much calm, in a mood to paint that."

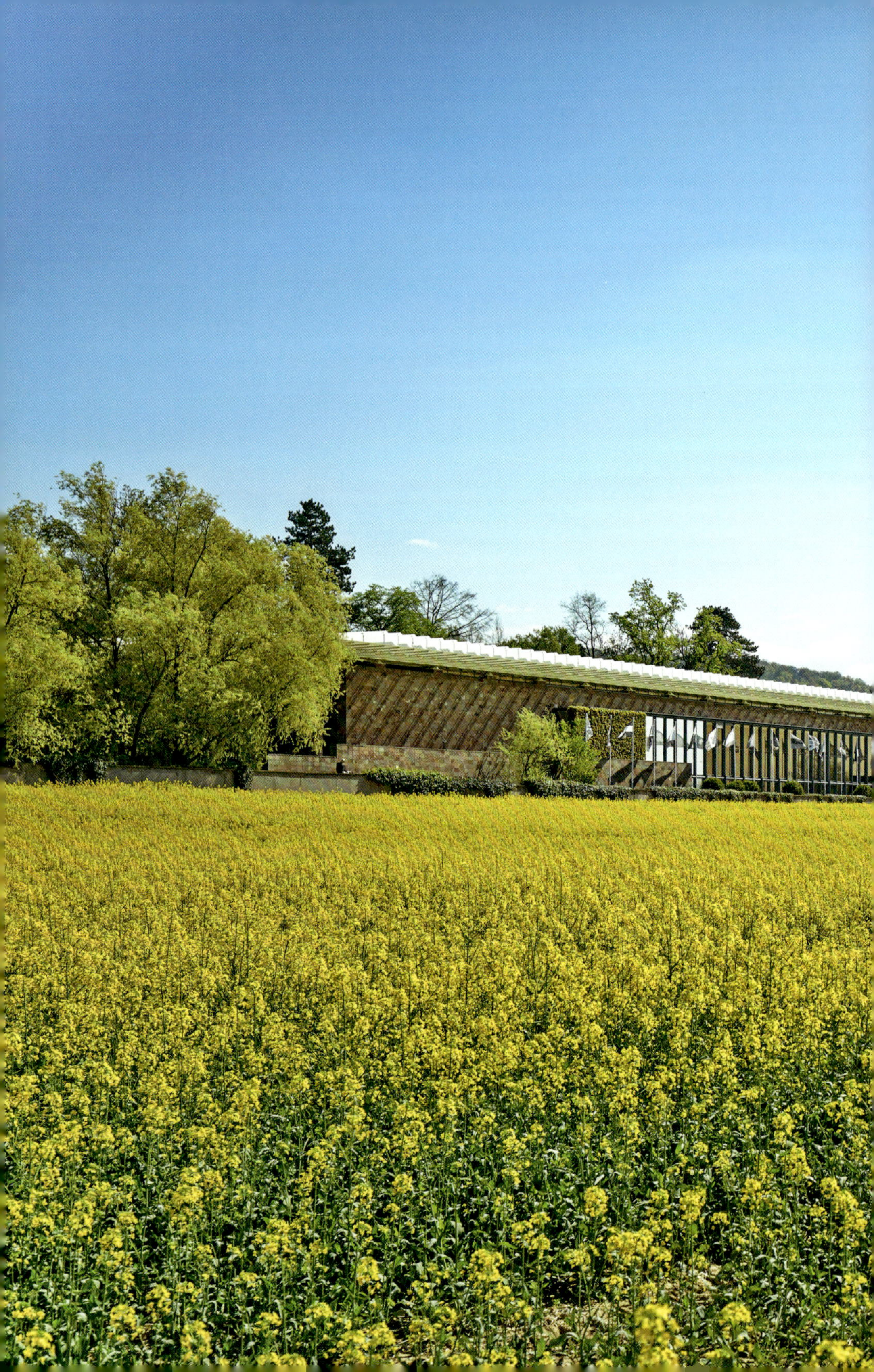

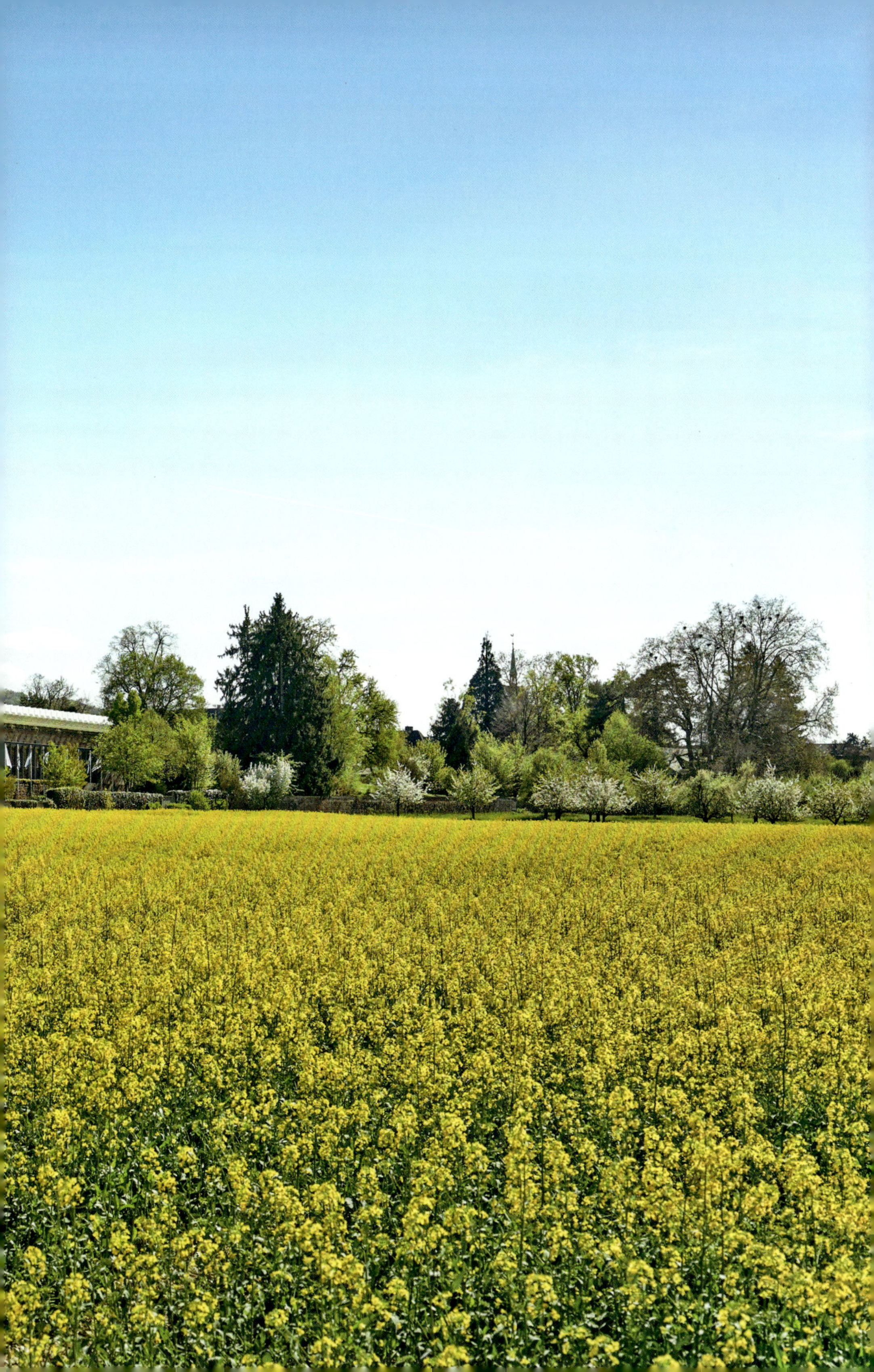

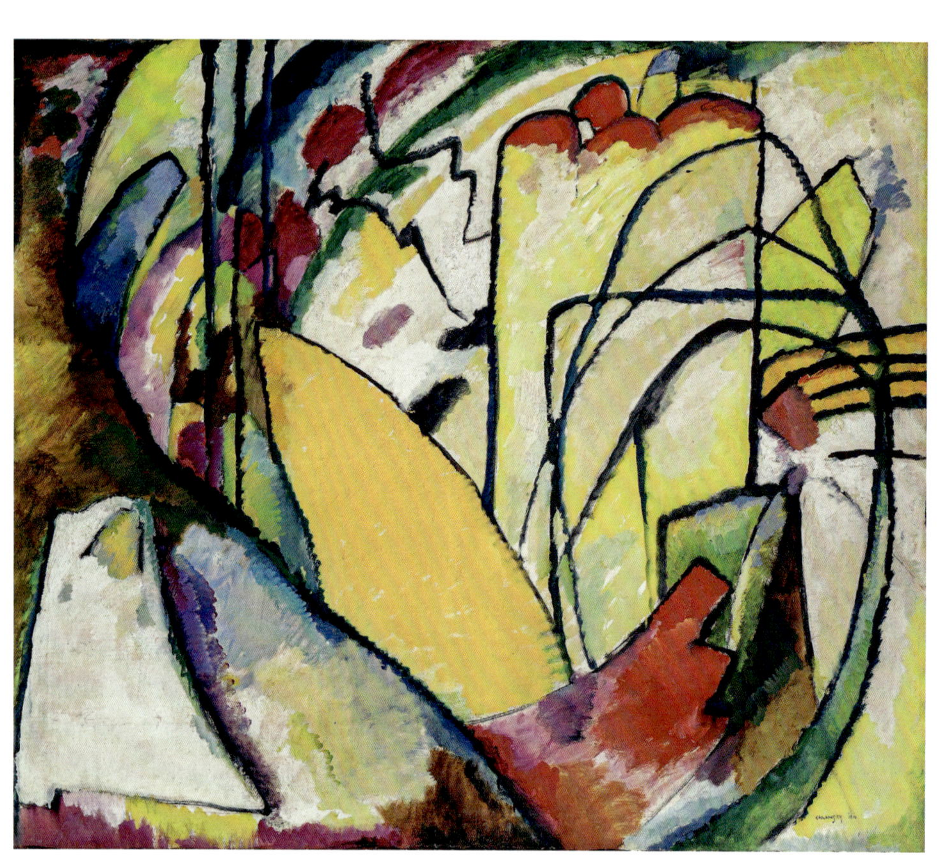

Wassily Kandinsky (1866–1944)

Improvisation 10, 1910

Oil on canvas, 120 × 140 cm

The Russian-German painter Wassily Kandinsky is considered one of the first artists to create fully abstract pictures. His urge to combine art, science, religion, and philosophy marks him out as a modern universalist.

Improvisation 10 is one of the key works in the Beyeler Collection and occupies a special place in its history. In 1997, Ernst Beyeler recalled: "At that time, I was still right at the beginning. I had seen a few [pictures] and was familiar with the literature, but this [work] took my breath away."

The degree of abstraction in Kandinsky's *Improvisation 10* is surprisingly high, and still gives rise to differing interpretations. Is the painting to be seen as a free color improvisation, or as a landscape, populated by human figures, whose glowing colors lead the viewer into the depths of the picture space? The artist himself wrote in 1904 in a letter to Gabriele Münter: "But the content should never be too clear or too one-sided. The more one leaves to be guessed at and interpreted, the better." For this painting, Kandinsky took figurative elements from previous works and developed them further, combining the expressive arabesque patterns of Art Nouveau with the exuberant colors of the Fauves to create a new formal language that merges space, color, and line. The black lines establish the rhythm, framing the blocks of bright color and organizing the picture in different spatial layers.

Aside from pointing to Kandinsky's interest in music, the title speaks above all of his search for an abstract visual language. In his "Improvisations," inner visions, thoughts, and ideas are transposed into a pictorial structure. The focus is no longer on the motif, but on the elements of creativity and expression, and their effects that unfold in the picture. In *Improvisation 10*, Kandinsky thus attains the sublime: the new picture arising from inner necessity, or the "spiritual in art."

Henri Matisse (1869–1954)

Nu bleu I | Blue Nude I, 1952
Gouache painted paper cut-outs
on paper on canvas, 106.3 × 78 cm

Henri Matisse is one of the twentieth century's truly outstanding artists. He redefined painting through formal reduction and by liberating color from the object. His innovative achievements in painting, drawing, and sculpture in the earlier phases of his career are reprised in his late series of *gouaches découpées*, or gouache cut-outs, which uniquely combine the three artistic media in which he had previously worked. He described the process of making these works as "Drawing with scissors: Cutting directly into vivid color reminds me of the direct carving of sculptors." At the time, Matisse was approaching the end of his life, with illness taking its toll, but nevertheless achieved a remarkable breakthrough with a completely new means of expression that became a summation of his life's work. Accordingly, the cut-outs stand at the center of the extensive holdings of Matisse's art in the Beyeler Collection. The simple yet highly complex technique enabled the artist to make subtle use of the colored forms in a way that is at once precise and playful. The "Blue Nudes," a series of four variations on the same theme, originally conceived as partial motifs for Matisse's monumental cut-out *La perruche et la sirène*, are among the artist's best-known works in this medium. *Nu bleu I*, the delicate yet imposing depiction of a crouching woman, is assembled from several parts, but looks as if it were created in a single virtuoso movement.

Matisse cut out the parts of the blue silhouette and assembled them, without using any perspective techniques, so that the impression of volume and depth arises directly from the surface. In terms of form and composition, the white spaces between the colored sections are almost as significant as the elements of the figure. With only a single color, and through contours alone, Matisse managed to endow the figure with expressiveness and charisma, evoking a mood of self-absorption combined with a serene sensuality.

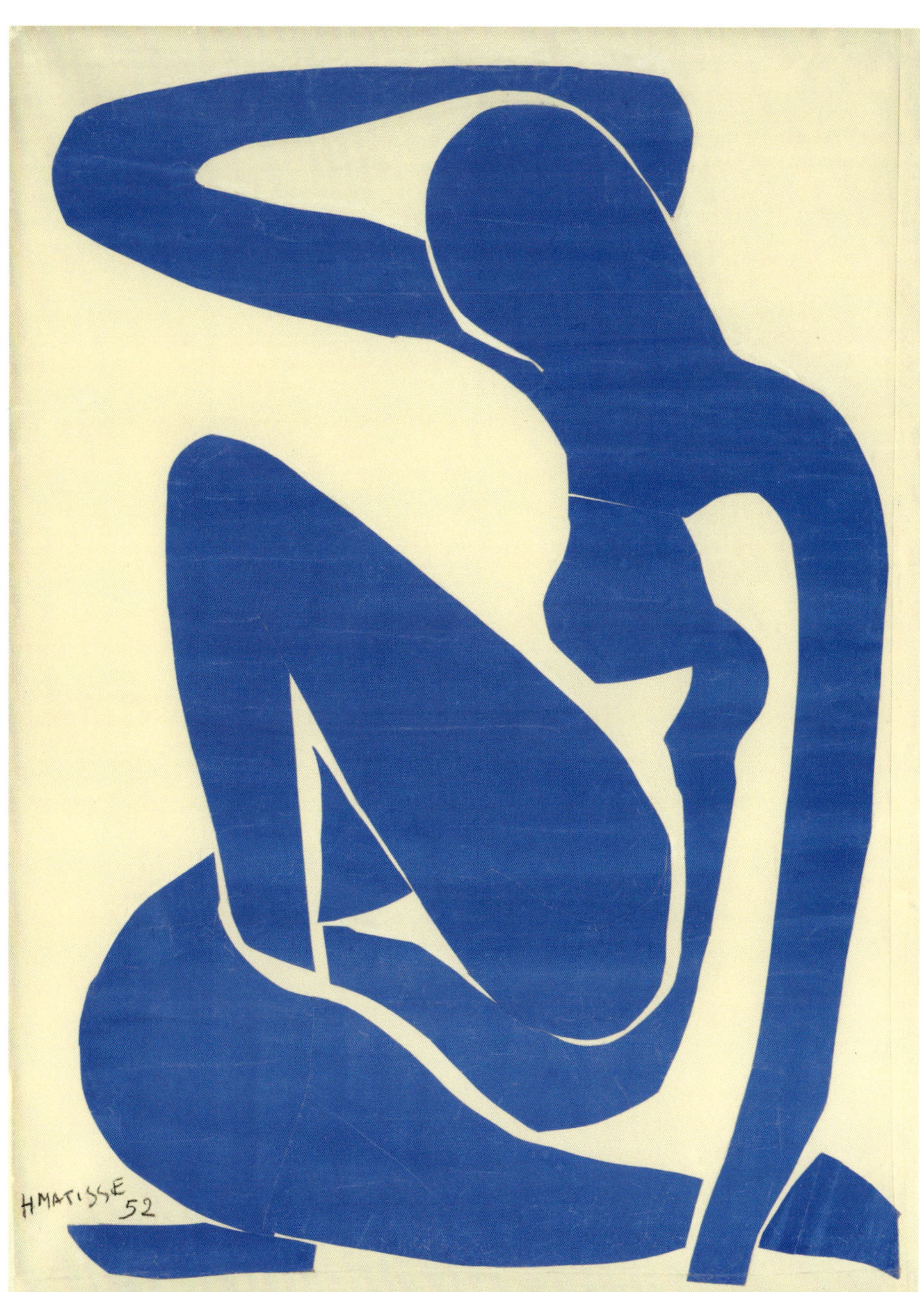
H MATISSE
52

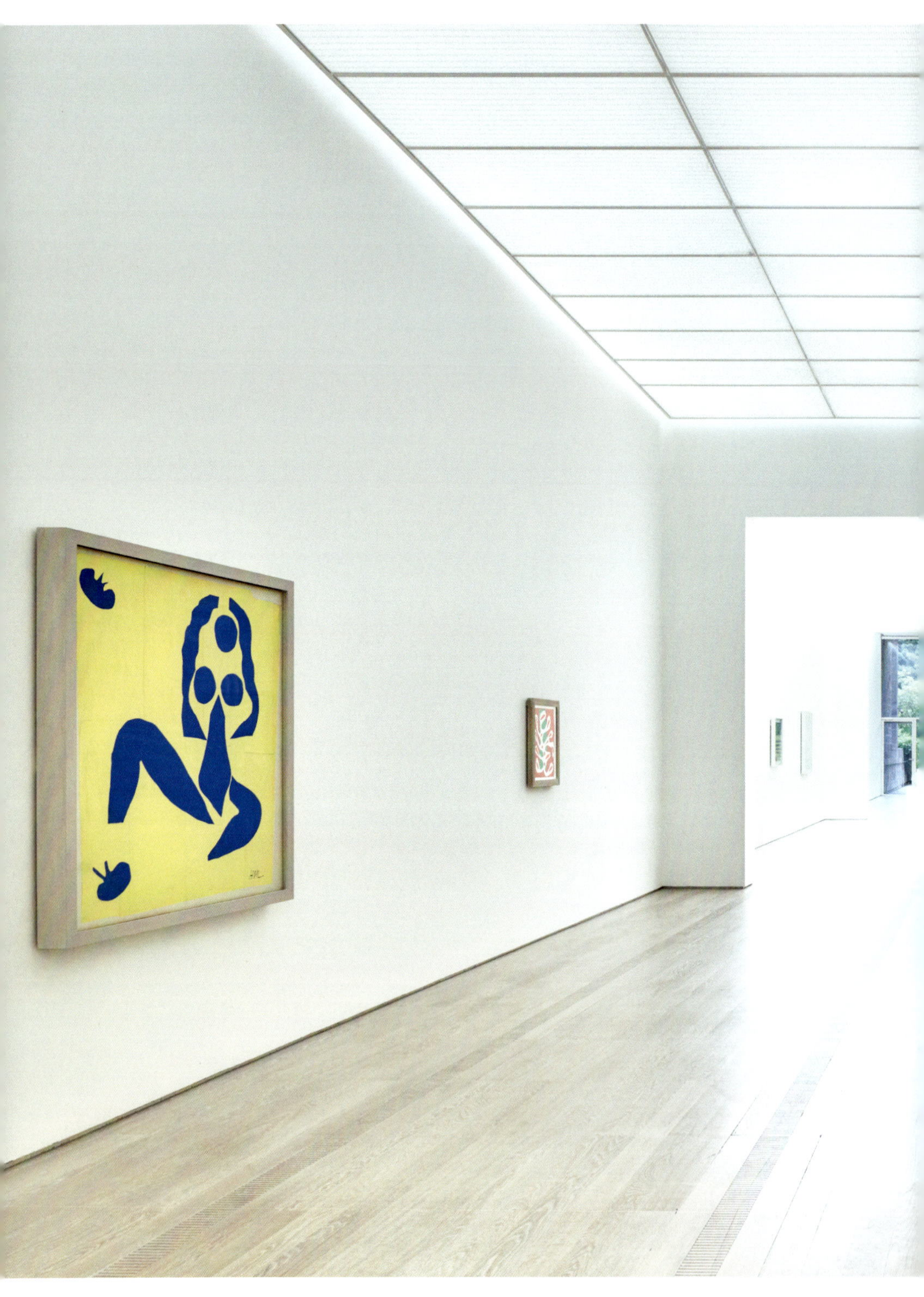

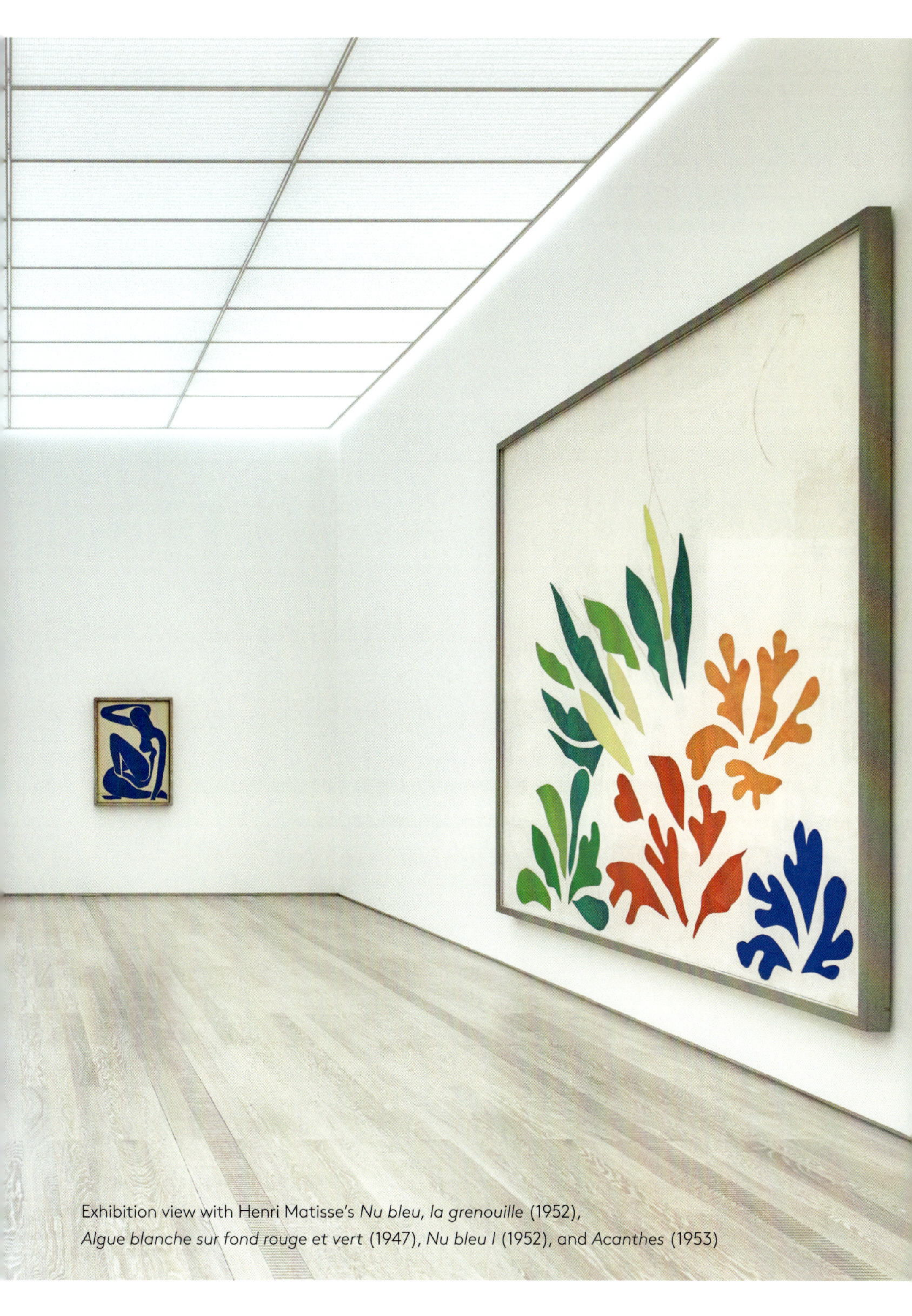

Exhibition view with Henri Matisse's *Nu bleu, la grenouille* (1952), *Algue blanche sur fond rouge et vert* (1947), *Nu bleu I* (1952), and *Acanthes* (1953)

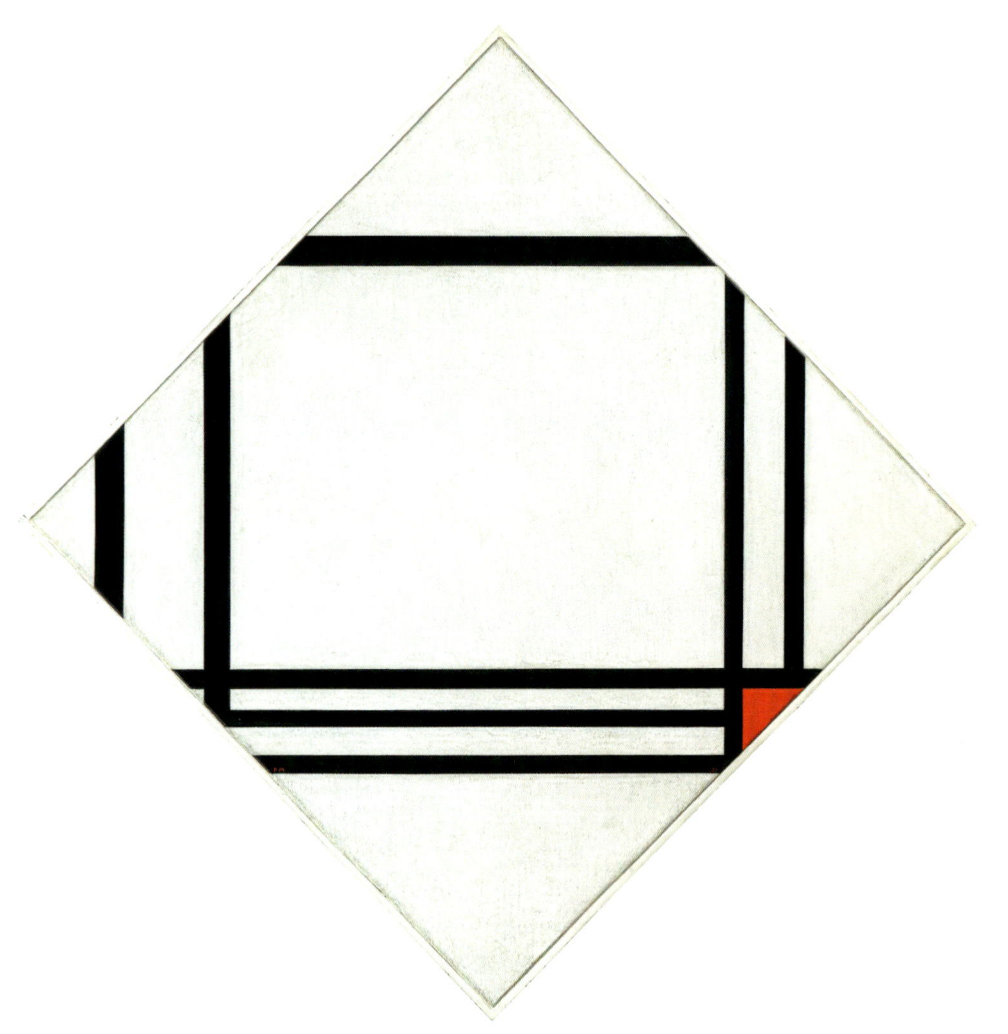

Piet Mondrian (1872–1944)

Lozenge Composition with Eight Lines and Red (Picture No. III), 1938
Oil on canvas, diagonals 141.5 cm

The collection of Ernst and Hildy Beyeler includes seven works by the Dutch painter Piet Mondrian, more than any other Swiss museum. This group of paintings, in which Mondrian's development from figuration to abstraction is especially apparent, begins with Cubist works from 1910 on and ends with a late lozenge picture made in 1938. Starting in the early 1920s, the artist embraced an entirely nonfigurative visual language, working in a style that he called Nieuwe Beelding, or Neo-Plasticism. His abstract pictures, created from the endless possible combinations of a white ground with black lines and the primary colors, yellow, red, and blue, established him as a defining figure in modern art.
Mondrian regarded abstraction as a process of approximation to absolute truth and beauty through light and reflections and the shaping of space, plane, and structure. His influence was felt not only in twentieth-century art but also in design, architecture, fashion, and pop culture.
Lozenge Composition with Eight Lines and Red is one of Mondrian's familiar square canvases turned onto one corner. The rectangular grid of vertical and horizontal lines, combined with a field of red, has the appearance of a detail from a much larger whole that could extend into infinity. This is a manifestation of Mondrian's ambition to grasp and embody every area of visible and invisible life in his abstract compositions. His forms are not geometrically measured, but freely composed, with almost no preliminary drawing. He worked at length on *Lozenge Composition with Eight Lines and Red*, in a process of continual revision and overpainting, until he found what he considered the perfect balance.

Constantin Brancusi (1876–1957)

L'oiseau | The Bird, 1923/1947

Marble and limestone, 121 × 27.5 × 26.7 cm

Constantin Brancusi's bird variations, comprising a group of around forty works, are among the most iconic sculptures of the twentieth century. The theme of the bird, in endless new versions and materials, recurs throughout the oeuvre of the celebrated Romanian-born artist, who lived in Paris from 1904 on. Starting with his first sculpture, *Maiastra*, from 1910–12, which addresses a figure based on Romanian folk mythology, Brancusi's ongoing reflection on the image of the bird in flight continued until the late 1940s. "All my life I have sought the essence of flight. Flight! What bliss!" the artist said, and this abiding interest gave rise to a body of work that hovers uniquely between figuration and abstraction.

The sculpture *L'oiseau* in the Beyeler Collection, executed in polished light-gray marble, is one of the works to which the artist probably devoted the most care and effort. He began working on the marble sculpture in 1923 and completed it more than two decades later, in 1947. Standing on a two-part pedestal that combines cruciform and zigzag-shaped elements, the slender, towering figure of the bird can be rotated on its own axis by means of an ingenious mechanism in the core of its limestone base, a unique feature of the Beyeler sculpture within this group of works by Brancusi. The bird's body, with its smoothly polished surface, tapers upward in a streamlined form, reminiscent of the movement of a bird as it takes flight and gathers speed. The veining of the marble, consciously harnessed by the artist, has a softening effect, mitigating the starkness and severity of the figure. The white veins also suggest the appearance of wings. Yet these few characteristic bird-like features suffice, as Brancusi's restrained and idealized sculptures are aimed at conveying the essence of flight, instead of reproducing the bird's physical being in naturalistic terms.

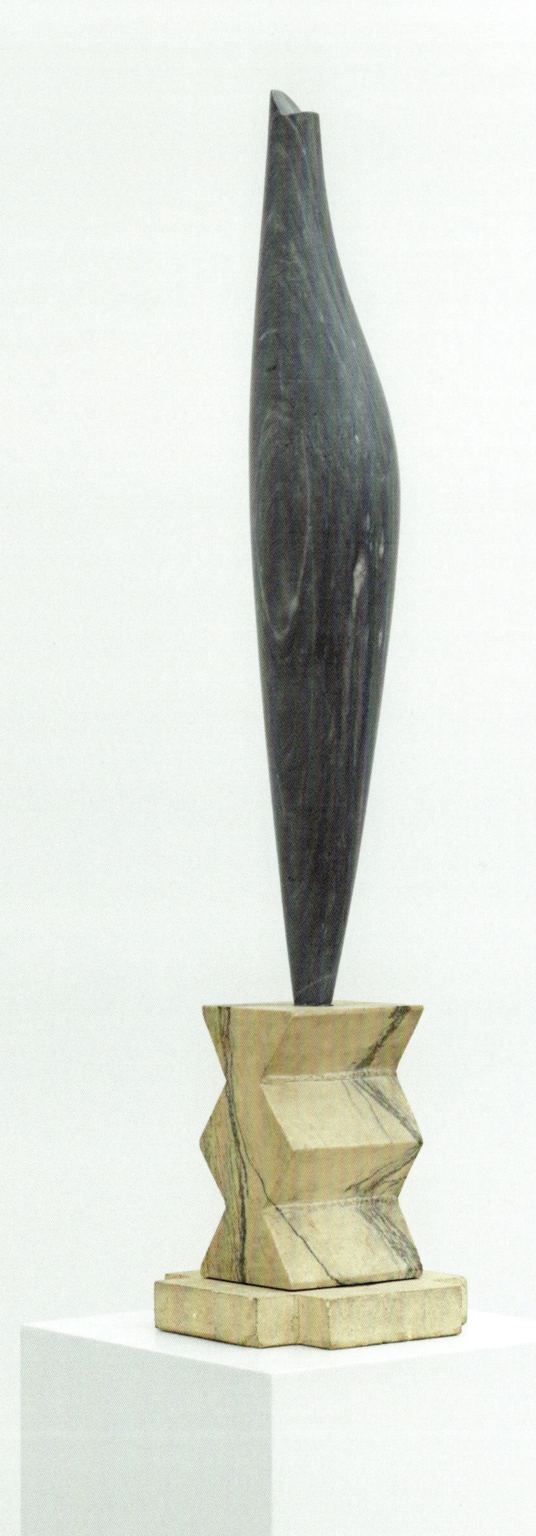

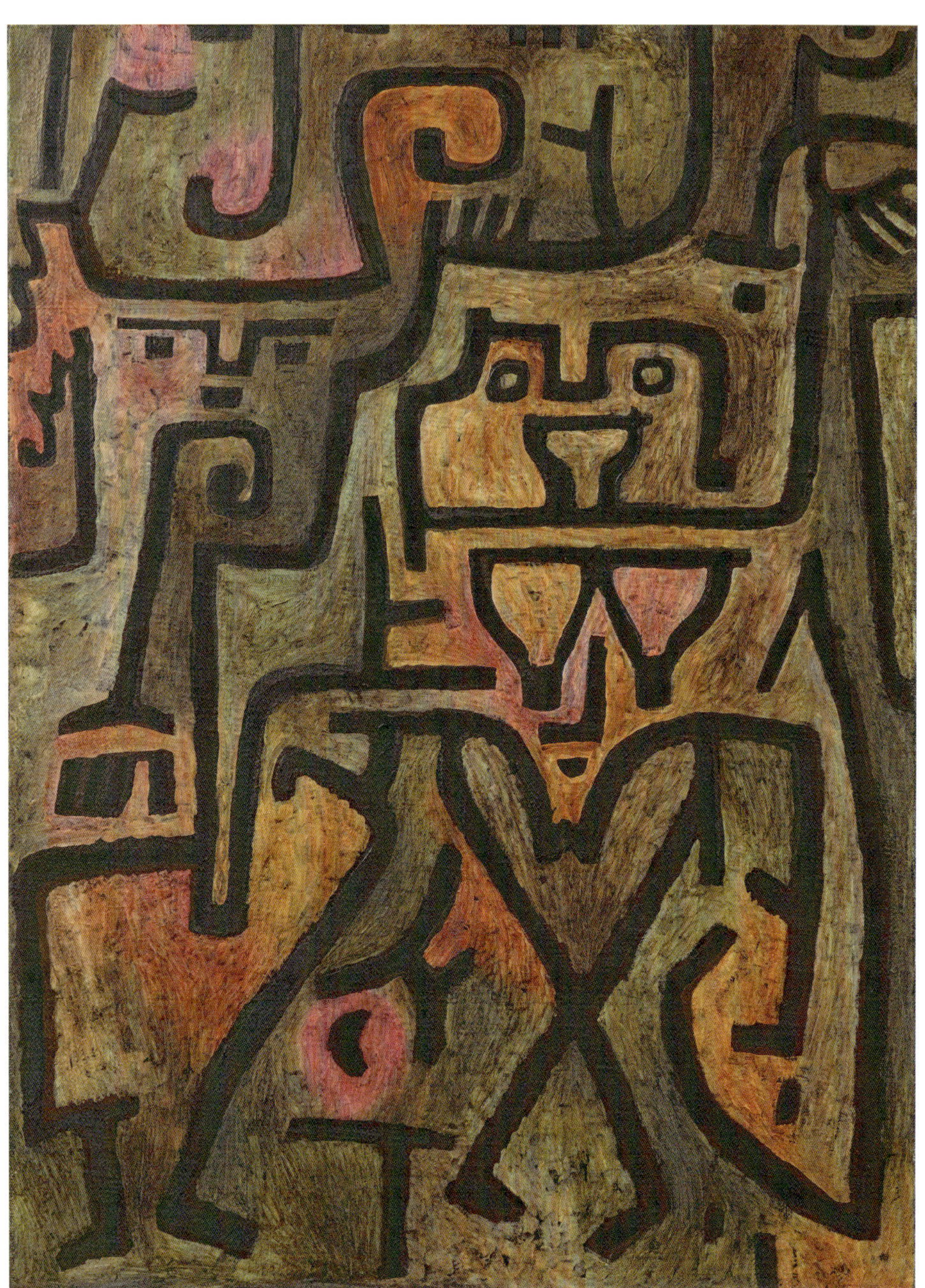

Paul Klee (1879–1940)

Wald-Hexen | Forest Witches, 1938

Oil on paper on burlap, 99 × 74 cm

Paul Klee is represented in the Beyeler Collection with twenty works from various phases of his oeuvre. A primary focus is on the artist's late work, with its exceptional visual language. *Wald-Hexen* was painted in the final years of Klee's life, in Switzerland, after his enforced return from Germany when the Nazis seized power. Born near Bern, Klee had spent most of his adult life in Germany and had held teaching posts at the Bauhaus and the Academy of Fine Arts in Düsseldorf.

Wald-Hexen is one of Klee's largest compositions. It appears to show a detail from a structure that extends far beyond the margins of the painting. Thick black lines animate the picture surface with ornamental rhythms. The resultant interstitial spaces are filled with short, dense brushstrokes in colors that range from beige, olive, and brown to orange and pink as well as blue. The application of the dappled paint, following the sweep of the dark lines, creates the effect of a relief. There is no real separation between foreground and background.

The picture's title is an invitation to read the dense thicket of lines in figurative terms. Closer inspection reveals the forms of faces and bodies, with breasts, legs, arms, hands, and hair. Klee may have found inspiration in the term *hagzissa*, the medieval origin of *Hexe* (witch), denoting a creature that lives between bushes and tree branches. The particular spelling of the title, yoking together the words *Wald* (forest) and *Hexen* as equivalent parts of a composite whole, is reflected in the blurring of visual distinctions between figures and foliage in the picture. In a further sense, *Wald-Hexen* poses a fundamental question about the conditions under which pictorial elements become signs or symbols that communicate something beyond just their given color and form. This interest in the relationship between image, sign, and text is generally characteristic of Paul Klee's oeuvre.

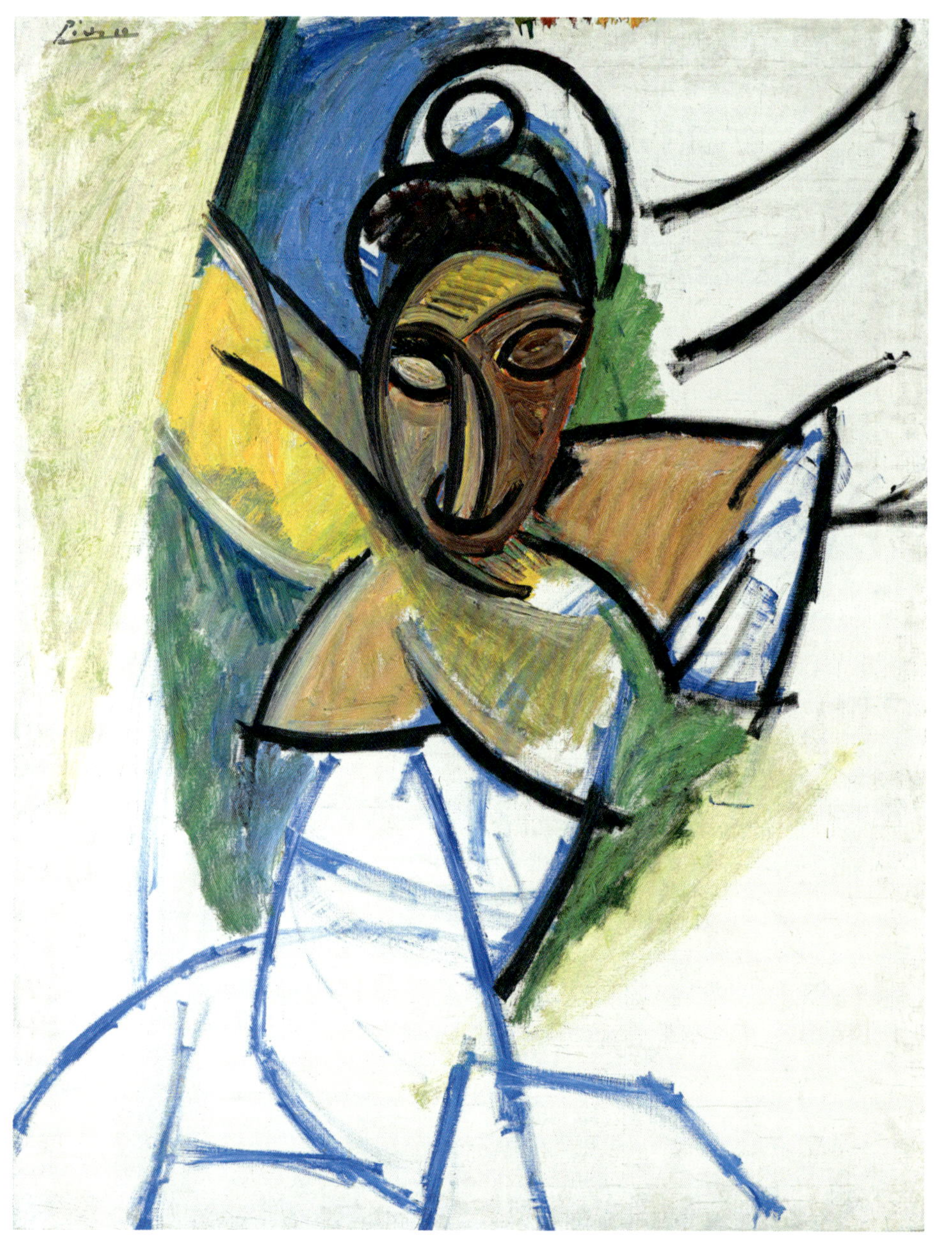

Pablo Picasso (1881–1973)

Femme (Époque des "Demoiselles d'Avignon")
Woman ("Demoiselles d'Avignon" Period), 1907
Oil on canvas, 119 × 93.5 cm

With his inexhaustible fund of pictorial ideas, Pablo Picasso had a deeper impact on twentieth-century art than almost any other artist. The Fondation Beyeler has one of the world's largest high-quality Picasso collections, comprising over thirty of his works. It also holds more works by Picasso than by any other modern artist, and thus offers a broad panorama of Picasso's oeuvre—from 1907, the year he created his revolutionary early painting *Les Demoiselles d'Avignon*, through the 1930s and 1940s, with characteristic pictures such as *Le sauvetage* and several depictions of Dora Maar, to the late works of the 1960s.
The making of *Les Demoiselles d'Avignon*, the pioneering work that initiated Cubism, involved an exceptionally long and arduous search for form. The process of creating the picture extended over several months, beginning in 1906, when Picasso made numerous preliminary studies on paper, cardboard, and canvas. *Femme*, from 1907, also originated in conjunction with *Les Demoiselles d'Avignon*. In an entirely innovative way, the sketch-like painting depicts a nude female figure with upraised arms, in a pose that remains ambivalent. Wearing the cap of a sailor or sea-captain and with her hair possibly gathered in a chignon, the woman reclines in front of a yellow curtain that is drawn to one side. Her face, painted with bold brushstrokes, looks like a woodcut. It is also reminiscent of the African masks that were prized by modern artists throughout Europe at the time, who had discovered the particular expressive impact of these artifacts and were using them as inspiration for their own creativity. While the woman's face as well as her arms and breasts are fully painted and clearly defined by black lines, the lower body is merely suggested with a few fleeting streaks of blue. Although *Femme* has the appearance of a study, the picture has the dynamism and expressive power of a finished work.

Max Ernst (1891–1976)

Fleurs de neige | Snow Flowers, 1929

Oil on canvas, 130 × 130 cm

Although Surrealist art is not a dominant focus in the collection of Ernst and Hildy Beyeler, Max Ernst is an exception: he is prominently represented with several pictures and sculptures from various phases of his career. The earliest of the paintings, with the poetic title *Fleurs de neige*, testifies to Ernst's preoccupation with a form of natural history in which the artist approached the subject from a personal, imaginative viewpoint, beyond scientific theories of nature and evolution. The work was created in Paris, where he settled in 1922 after leaving Germany, and became a central exponent of Surrealism. *Fleurs de neige* belongs to a series of fantasy "flower landscapes," in which the floral elements emerge from all manner of other natural forms—evoking, in the case of this work, a connection and transformation of flowers and snowflakes, two natural phenomena that are entirely distinct and unrelated. The composition is based on three geometric fields that suggest a landscape of hills under a night sky. At the rear, a small blue sphere hints at the shape of the planet Earth. Floating through this extraterrestrial cosmos, empty of human life, are strange multicolored flowers that appear partly frozen. Following his penchant for experimentation, the artist made these images using unusual methods, namely, the new scraping and rubbing techniques known as *grattage* and *frottage*. This resulted in a fascinating interplay of color layers and structures, with iridescent chromatic effects, leaving the viewer to wonder about the facture and texture of the painting's surface. Finally, on the lower right, a small picture within the picture, showing a family of birds, is inserted in the composition as the artist's personal emblem.

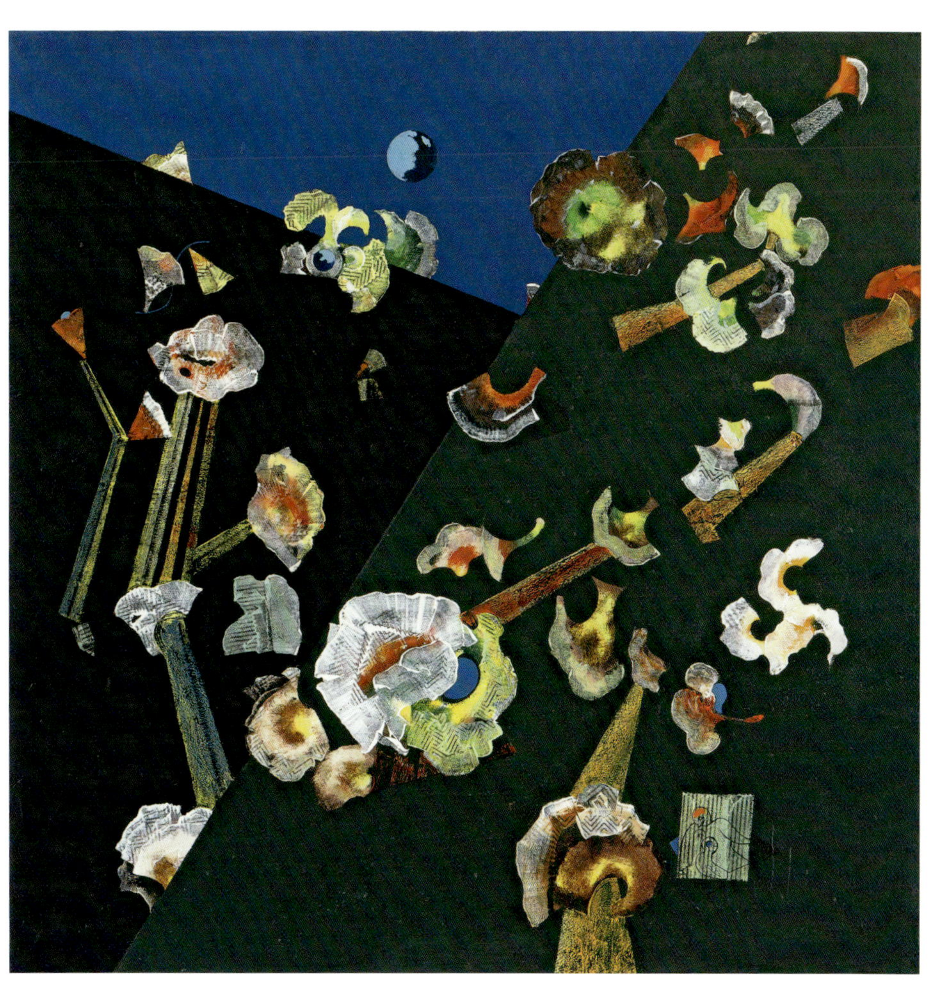

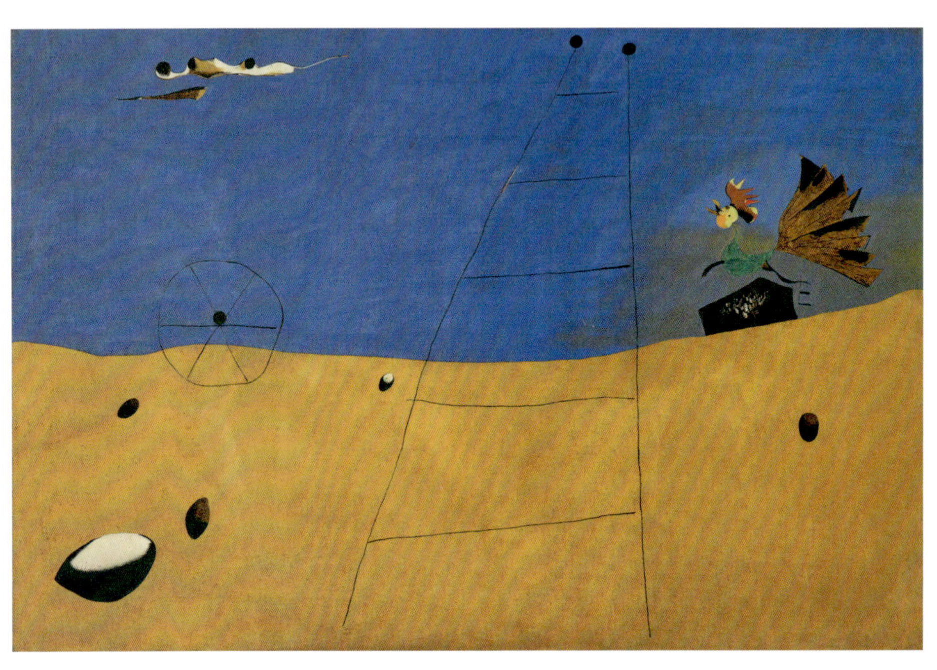

Joan Miró (1893–1983)

Paysage (Paysage au coq)

Landscape (Landscape with Rooster), 1927

Oil on canvas, 131 × 196.5 cm

Joan Miró had already achieved some early success as an artist in his home city of Barcelona before he moved to Paris and settled in the French capital in the early 1920s. There, at the center of the French art world, he spent several formative years as a member of the Surrealist circle around André Breton. From 1925 onward, the painter gradually abandoned his early figurative style in favor of a sparse pictorial language that combined Surrealism with abstraction. Subsequently, his work was characterized by an emphasis on the imaginary, the dreamlike, and the anecdotal. Together with artists such as Yves Tanguy and André Masson, he developed the idea of *peinture automatique*, by analogy with Breton's technique of automatic writing. The purpose of this method was no longer to depict the world of objects with realistic accuracy, but to activate the unconscious and translate it into pictures.

Paysage au coq exemplifies the style of Miró's early Surrealist work. The painting is part of a series, made in 1927, of "imaginary landscapes" in which a horizon line divides the horizontal-format picture surface into two monochrome fields of color. In *Paysage au coq*, the deep blue of the sky contrasts sharply with the brown earth tones. The two areas are connected by a ladder extending from the lower edge to the top of the canvas. The pastoral motifs were inspired by the area around Mont-roig del Camp in Catalonia, where Miró spent the summer months on his father's farm. The larger-than-life rooster on the right, perching on the ridge of a pitched roof, with its beak wide open, is painted in colors that probably allude to pre-Republican Spain, while the letter "E," dangling from the creature's leg, evokes the word *España*.

Miró's oeuvre teems with references to his Catalonian homeland and its folklore, in which the color blue has a particular significance. In the phase of his work between 1925 and 1927, blue is especially dominant. This is also apparent in *Peinture (Personnages: Les frères Fratellini)* (1927), which, with *Paysage au coq*, is the earliest of the seven works by Miró in the Beyeler Collection.

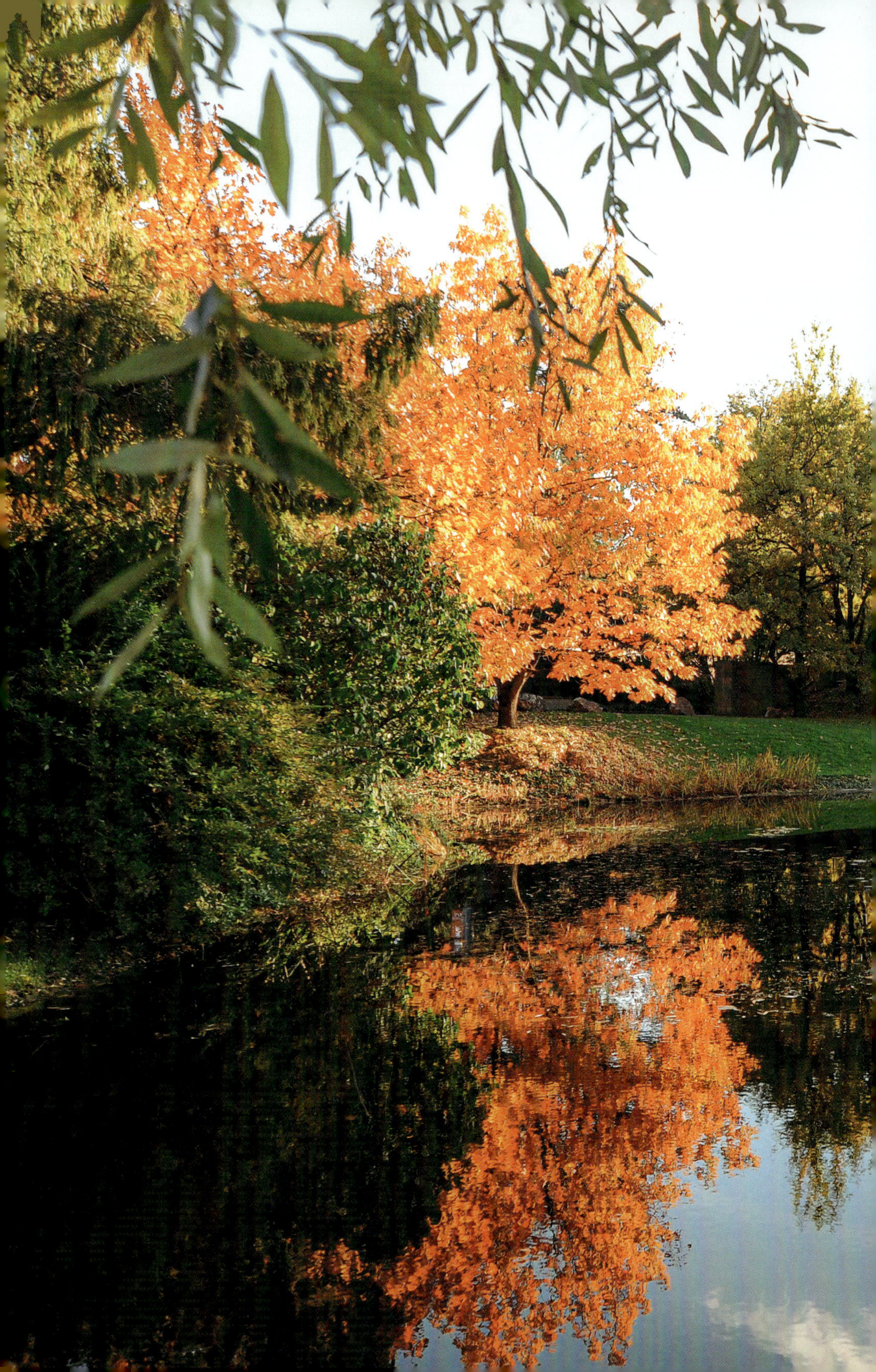

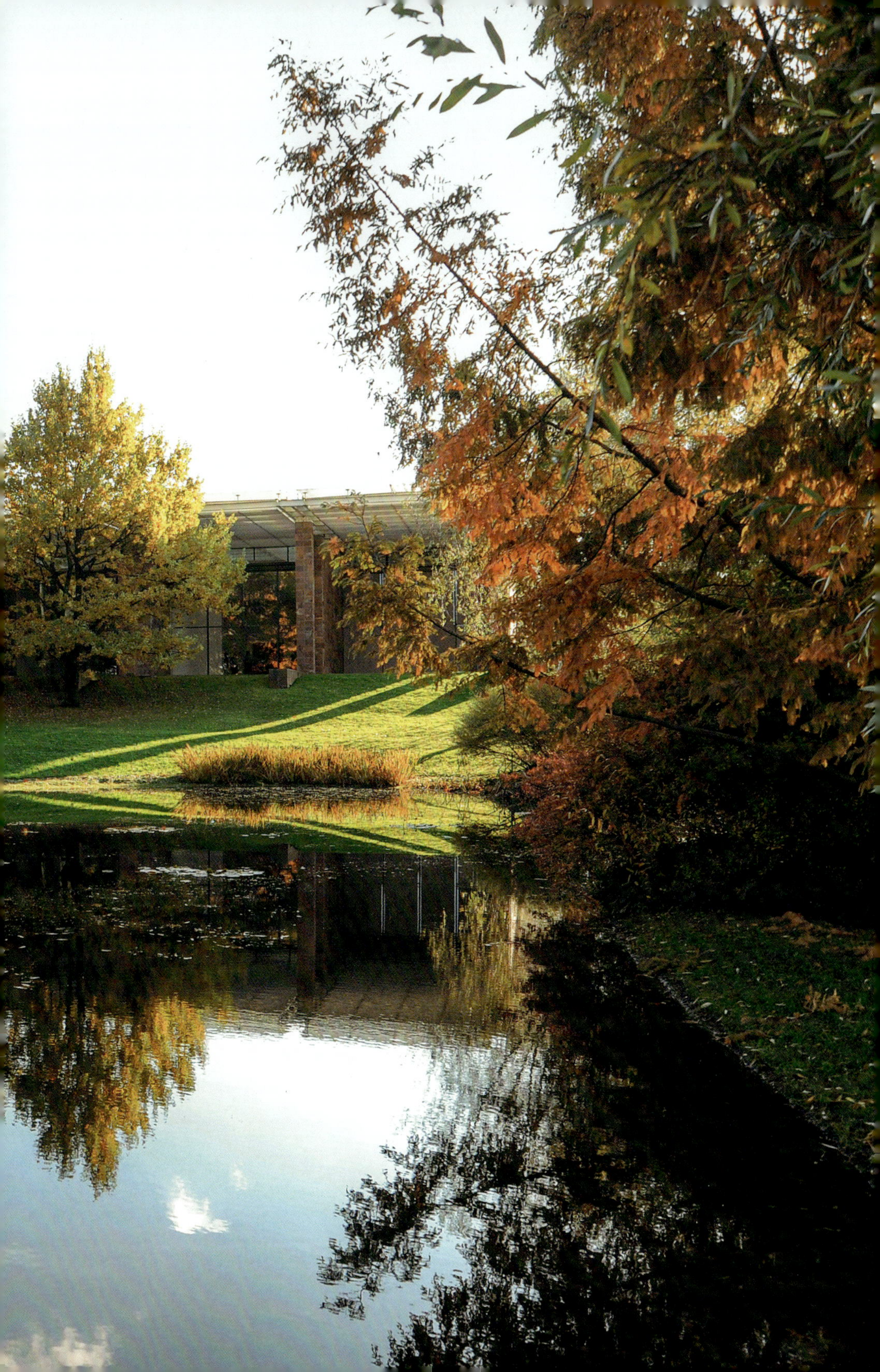

Alexander Calder (1898–1976)

The Tree, 1966

Steel, aluminum, and paint,
ca. 610 × 1070 × 520 cm

With his abstract mobile sculptures, Alexander Calder liberated sculpture from the traditional, static idea of the artwork. He is regarded as the foremost pioneer of kinetic art.

Calder came from a family of sculptors and attended the Art Students League in 1923–25. In Paris, where he lived from 1926 to 1933 and moved in avant-garde circles, he gravitated toward abstraction, experimenting with nonfigurative three-dimensional constructions of wire, wood, and sheet metal, equipped in some cases with motors. This culminated in the development of the mobile, moving in response to air currents, which became the basis for much of Calder's future work. His intuitive knowledge of scale was extremely useful in the construction of his increasingly complex and soon monumental sculptures.

One of these large-scale works is the standing mobile *The Tree*, from 1966, titled after its creation. With its striking form, the sculpture is an especially characteristic work in the Fondation Beyeler park, uniting Calder's idea of the mobile with his "stabiles," the second type of structure conceived by him. Here, the uneven triangular forms spread outward to support the anchoring of the trunk of the piece in the ground; attached to the top is a pivot bearing with a horizontal element like a balance scale. At either end of the scale, a delicately adjusted mobile structure with four steel "leaves" of unequal size is set in motion by the slightest breath of wind.

The Tree brings together the fundamental elements of Calder's oeuvre. His works seek a balance between gravity and weightlessness, reconciling chance with control. With the utmost precision and maximum lightness, they explore the possibilities of movement in space and create poetic forms of precarious equilibrium.

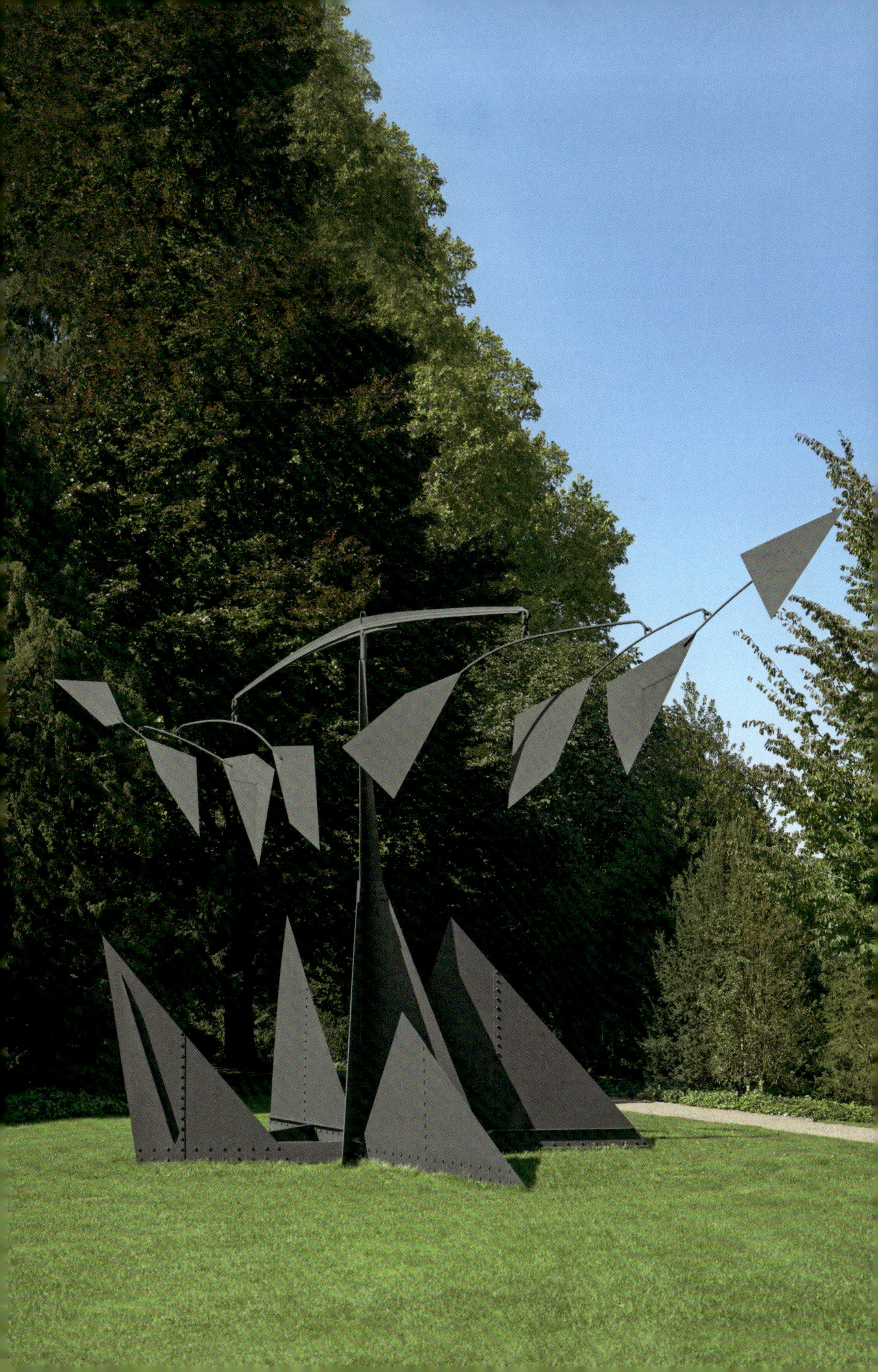

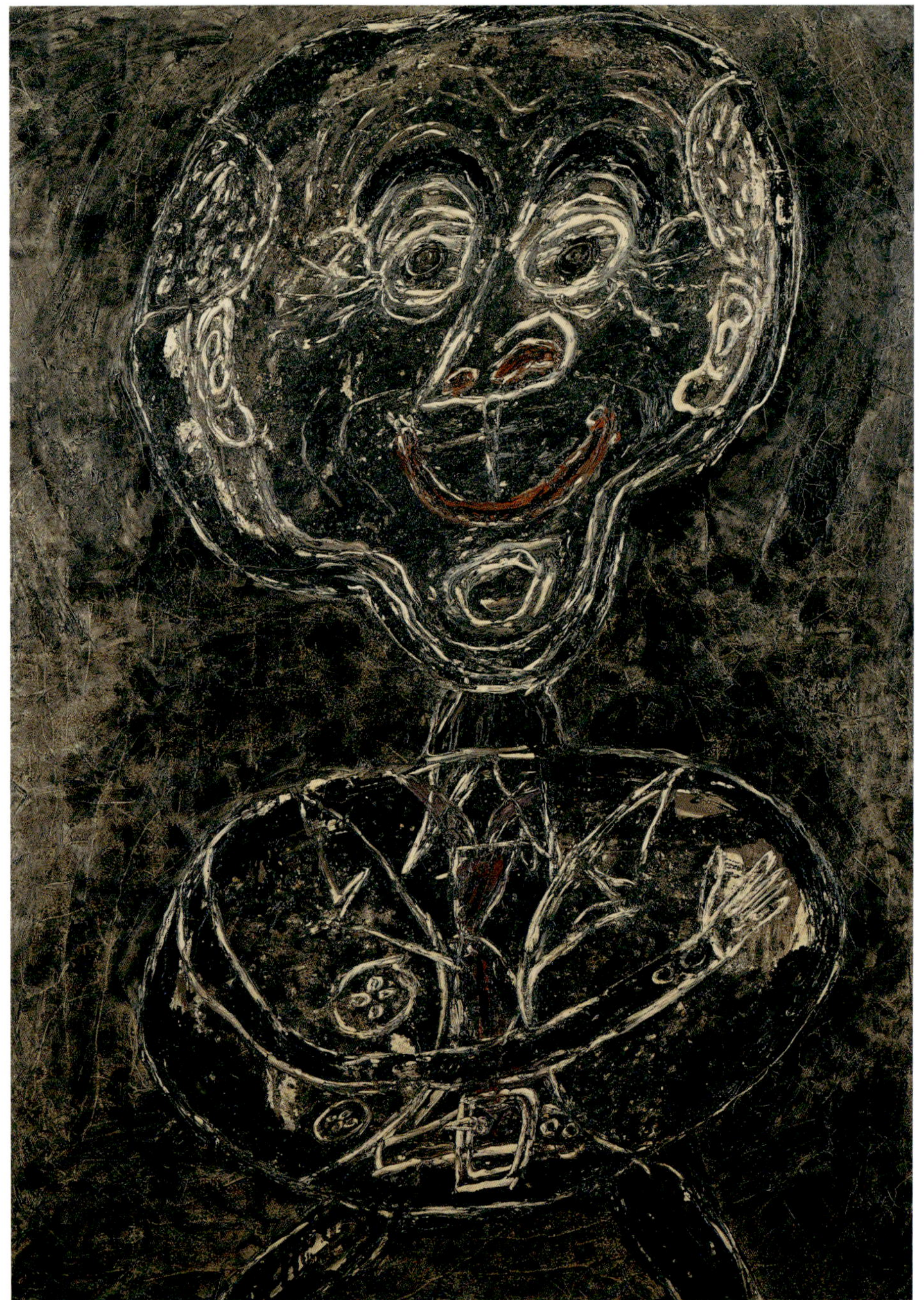

Jean Dubuffet (1901–1985)

Ponge feu follet noir

Ponge as Will-o'-the-Wisp, 1947

Oil and mixed media on canvas on hardboard, 132.5 × 99.5 cm

"People are more beautiful than they think they are. Long live their true face." This was the title of an exhibition of works by Jean Dubuffet that opened in October 1947 at the Galerie René Drouin in Paris. The show featured a group of portraits of writers, artists, and thinkers, including a depiction of the writer Francis Ponge (1899–1988), titled *Ponge feu follet noir*. In the summer of 1945, the wealthy American patron Florence Gould had commissioned Dubuffet to paint the guests at her weekly salon. The artist, who had given up his wine business just a few years earlier to, at the age of forty-one, devote himself to painting, set about the task with gusto. He spent several hours with his subjects, studying them very carefully, before returning to his studio to paint their portraits from memory. The works are neither conventional likenesses, nor mere caricatures. Dubuffet captured the essence of the model in a way that was categorically opposed to psychology and individuality, in accordance with his vision of an aesthetic that was beyond the traditional ideals of beauty enshrined in Western art. The above-mentioned exhibition title also stands in this context. Dubuffet found inspiration in graffiti, children's drawings, and the work of self-taught artists in psychiatric hospitals, for which he coined the term *art brut*, and which he himself collected. His rejection of traditional ideas about art is also reflected in his practice of experimenting with unusual materials, such as ashes, sand, and gravel.

As an art dealer, Ernst Beyeler was an important supporter of Dubuffet. The Beyeler Collection includes a total of twelve works from various phases of the artist's extremely rich and varied oeuvre.

Alberto Giacometti (1901–1966)

L'homme qui marche II | Walking Man II, 1960

Bronze, 188.5 × 29.1 × 111.2 cm

Perhaps the most famous of Alberto Giacometti's sculptures is *L'homme qui marche II*, a work that represents dynamism and movement. The male figure striding purposefully forward is condensed into a potent metaphor. Giacometti had originally envisioned the work as an outdoor sculpture for the Chase Manhattan Plaza in New York. The Beyeler Collection also includes versions of the other accompanying figures intended for the site.

Giacometti was convinced that a work of art might strive for perfection but was ultimately doomed to fail. What drove him onward was the thought that continual failure could lead to a higher level of understanding. The group of figures that was never installed at the planned location at the Chase Manhattan Plaza is an especially good example of this. From today's perspective, Giacometti did not fail: what he created here was a definition of space and movement via sculpture that remains fascinating, one that is variable and can be rearranged continually in different ways.

Between 1959 and 1960, Giacometti worked intensely on several versions of this work, eventually deciding to group the third and fourth version of a female figure with the second variant of the walking man, in combination with the rendering of a head with slightly upturned gaze. This suggests the act of looking at the constellation of the other figures: first, at the women, who recall antique stelae, but whose standing pose implies a tension, as if they were ready to stride off immediately; and second, at the man stepping out, with one foot firmly in front of the other.

How can an artist depict movement? This question preoccupied Giacometti, like so many other artists. After a visit to the cinema, he began to see movement as a succession of standstills. This is how the group should be seen: the seemingly disembodied, purely symbolic nature of the sculptures and the calculated roughness of their surfaces and contours, making them difficult to grasp, shows that standstill is a fleeting moment.

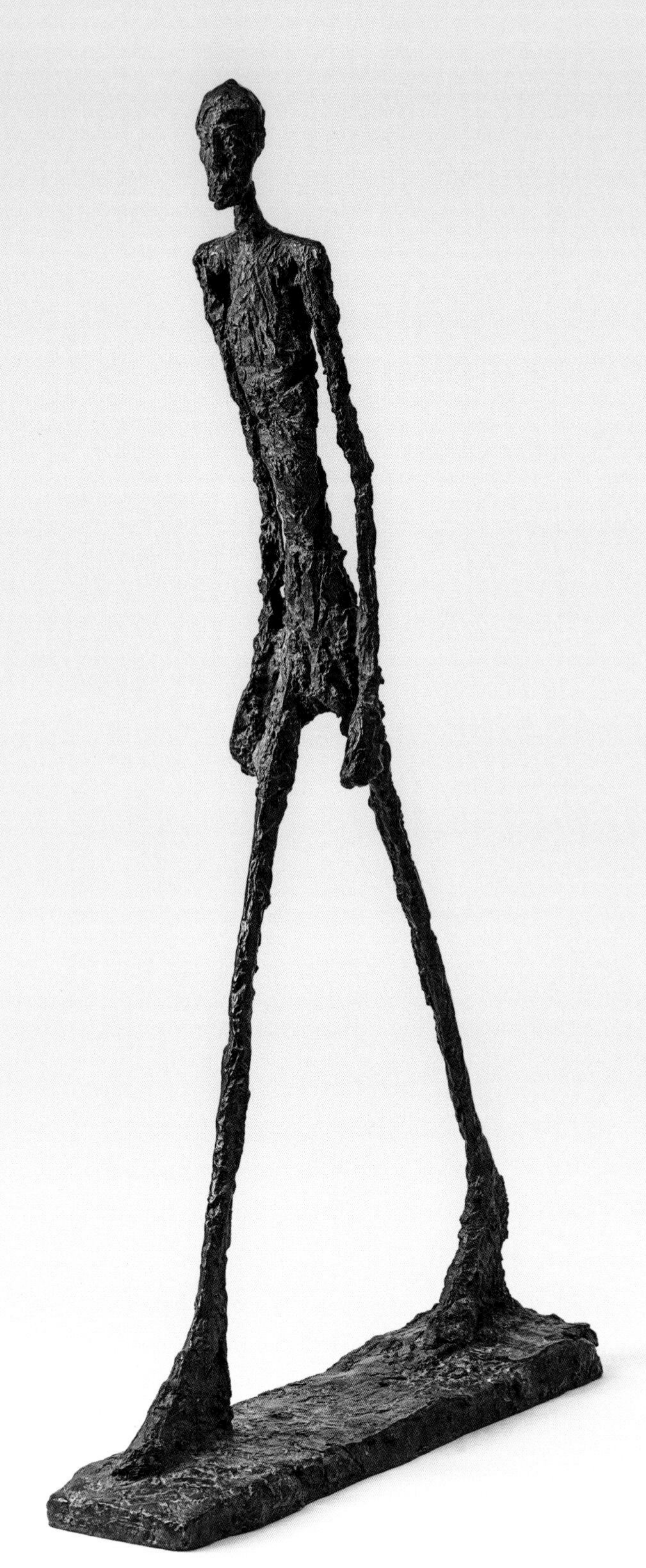

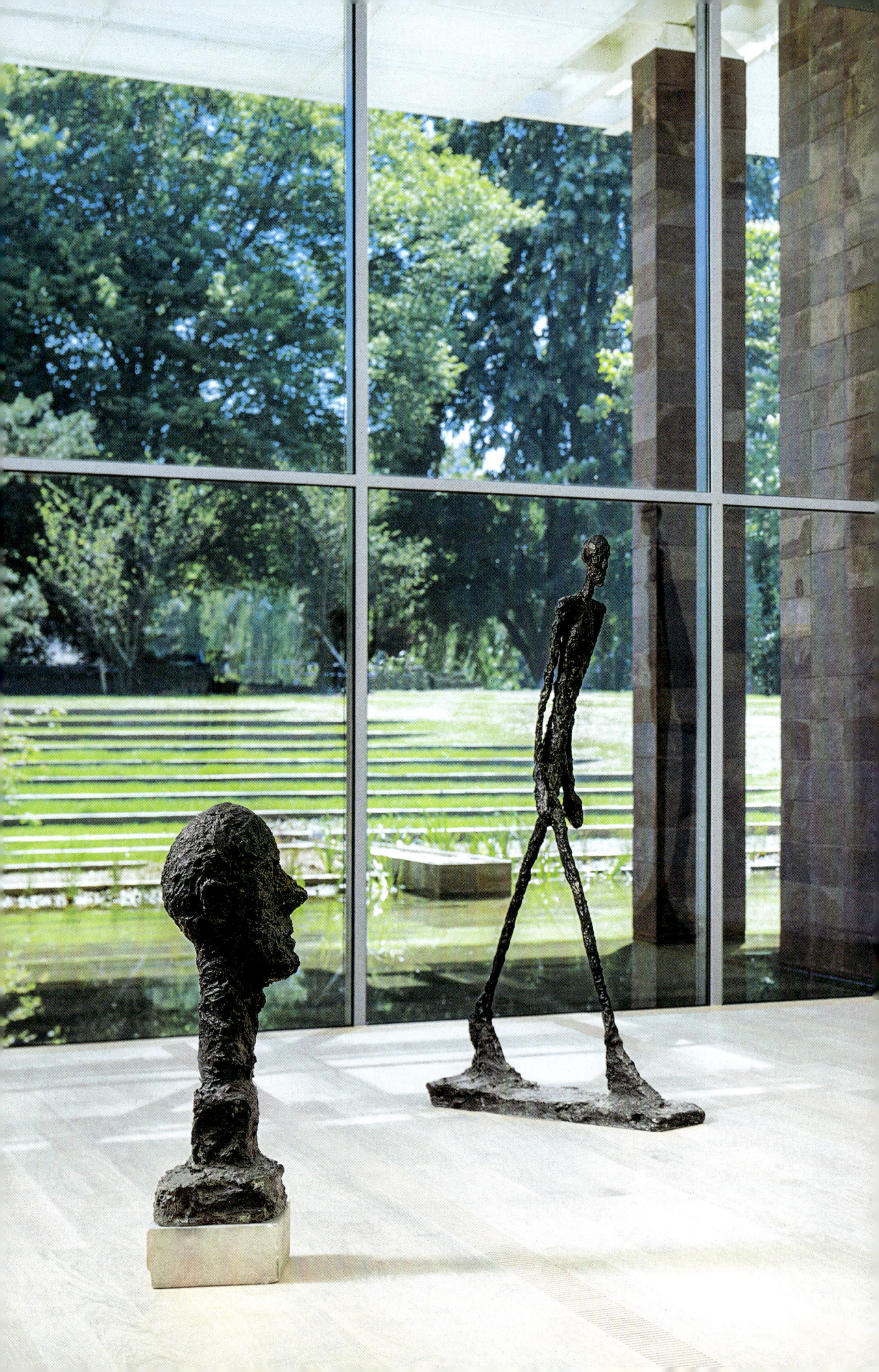

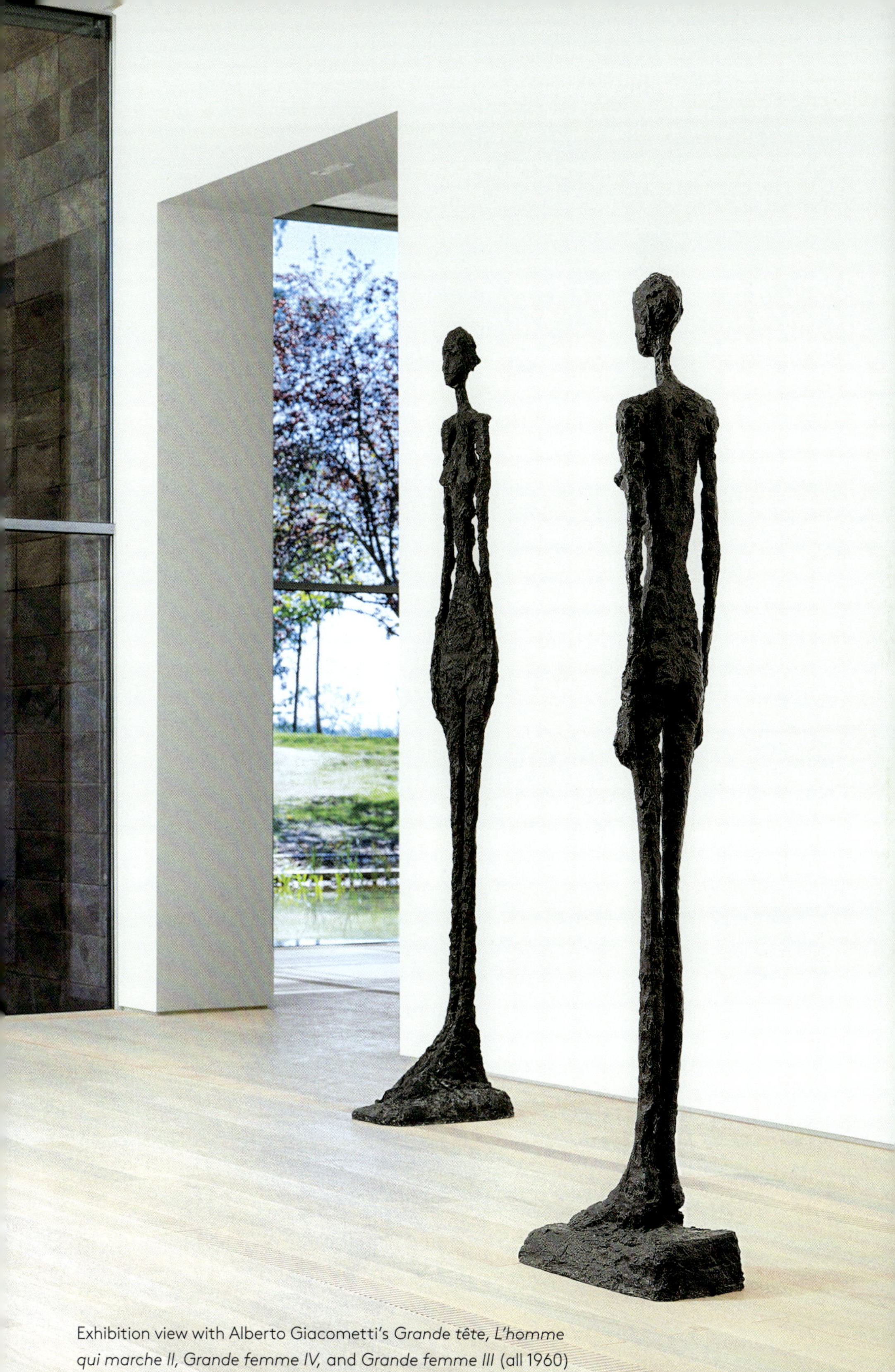

Exhibition view with Alberto Giacometti's *Grande tête*, *L'homme qui marche II*, *Grande femme IV*, and *Grande femme III* (all 1960)

Mark Rothko (1903–1970)

Untitled (Red, Orange), 1968

Oil on canvas, 233 × 176 cm

In 1972, Ernst and Hildy Beyeler's enthusiasm for Mark Rothko led them to acquire their first work by the artist for their own collection. The picture was *Untitled (Red, Orange)*, from 1968, a vertical-format composition in warm red and orange tones, in which two superimposed fields are set on a monochrome ground. The zones of color grow denser toward the center but soften and dissolve at the edges. This pulsating movement brings the color to life as a protagonist in the picture, creating an effect that is immediate and self-reflexive.

Rothko arrived at this compositional format as early as 1950 and adhered to it—with only a few exceptions—in all of his subsequent works, varying only the color combinations and the number of fields. Stripping art of its traditional narrative content, he declared the act of painting to be the real subject matter of the picture. Rothko was not the sole initiator of this revolution in art: in the late 1940s, the Western art world was set on its ear by a group of young New York artists who came to be known as the Abstract Expressionists. Today, Rothko is known as the creator of vibrant color field paintings that open the way for a meditative dialogue between the picture and the viewer.

The experience of seeing Rothko's paintings may seem intuitive, but their effect is meticulously calculated, with the intention of immersing the viewer in the color fields and eliciting an emotional response to their particular aura. To heighten the intensity of this encounter, Rothko insisted that his works be presented isolated from others in exhibitions. After his death, however, the paintings were sold individually. Four further major works by the artist were acquired for the Beyeler Collection and are now shown regularly as a unique ensemble in "Rothko Rooms."

Francis Bacon (1909–1992)

In Memory of George Dyer, 1971

Oil on canvas, triptych, 198 × 147.5 cm each

Francis Bacon's depiction of his former lover George Dyer takes up the format of the triptych, the religious pictorial tradition of the three-panel painting found in medieval altarpieces. The devotional purpose of the traditional triptych is echoed in this work, which is an act of commemoration. The suicide of Bacon's lover, in 1971, was the painful culmination of a relationship between the artist and his model that often took on an obsessive character. *In Memory of George Dyer* is a touching expression of emotional engagement with the death of a loved one.

The three images of George Dyer are situated at the margins of reality, in settings that appear surreal and dreamlike. The central panel shows a staircase dimly lit by a naked lightbulb. A bare arm, belonging to a shadowy figure in a dark suit, reaches out to insert a key in a door lock. The figure seems at once absent and present. The staircase functions as a place of transition, leaving it uncertain whether the figure is coming or going.

On the left, the shadowy figure is flanked by a depiction of Dyer as a boxer sinking to the floor. His face is distorted into a grimace, and parts of his body are dissolving. The surrounding space is almost entirely empty. Dyer's body has not yet fallen completely to the ground, but the fight is clearly lost, and it is too late to hope for a reversal. The curving line that formally connects the side panels and holds the composition together has the function, on a practical level, of the ropes around a boxing ring; but it also has the formal effect of anchoring the body in the pictorial space and supplying an element of stability.

The panel on the right shows Dyer as a picture within a picture, in the image reflected on the tabletop. Here, the curving line becomes a shelf on which the dead man's portrait rests. The mirror image seems to be peeling away in places or even dissolving altogether, alluding to the conflicted inner state of a person in deep distress.

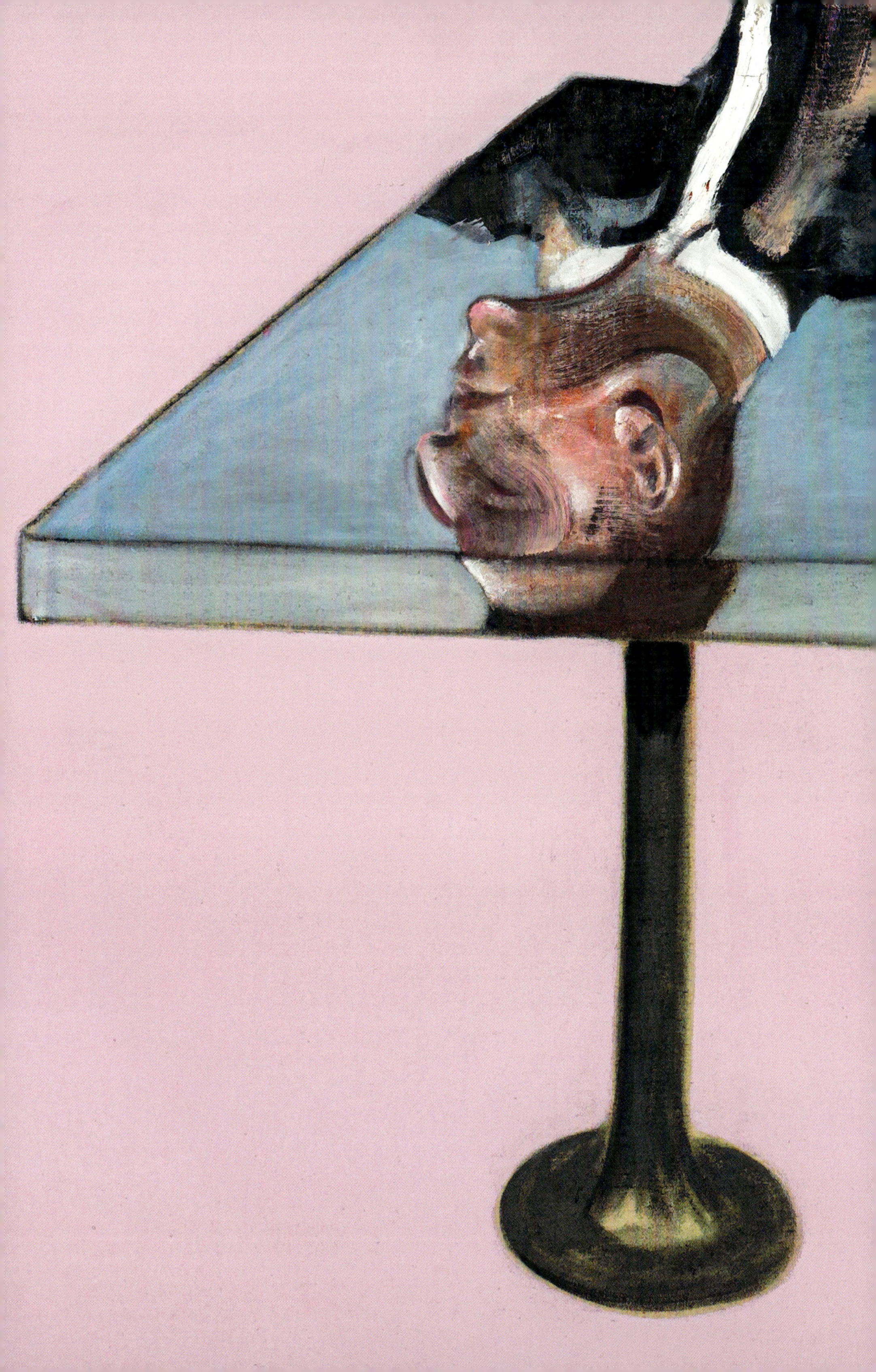

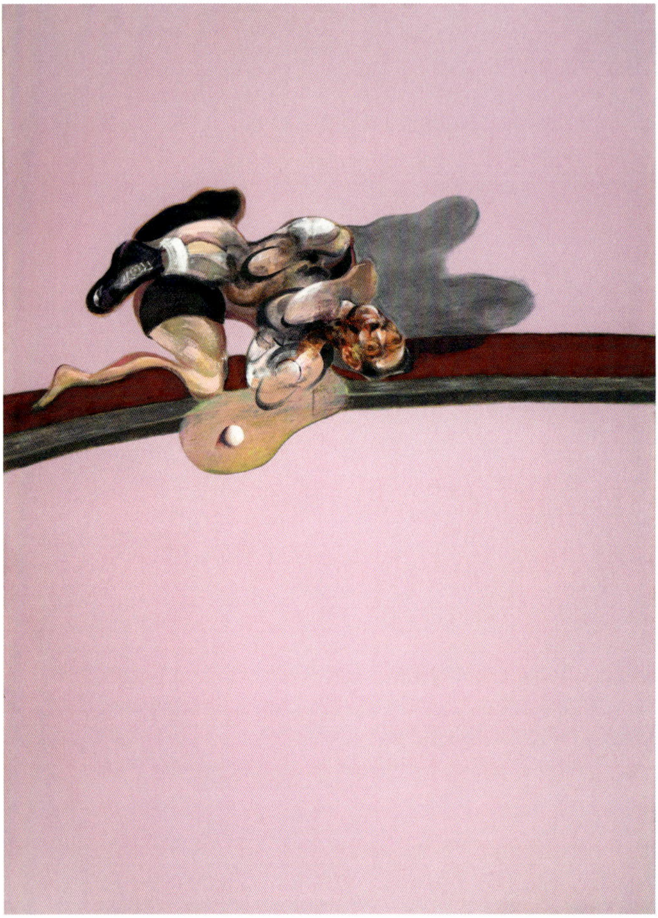

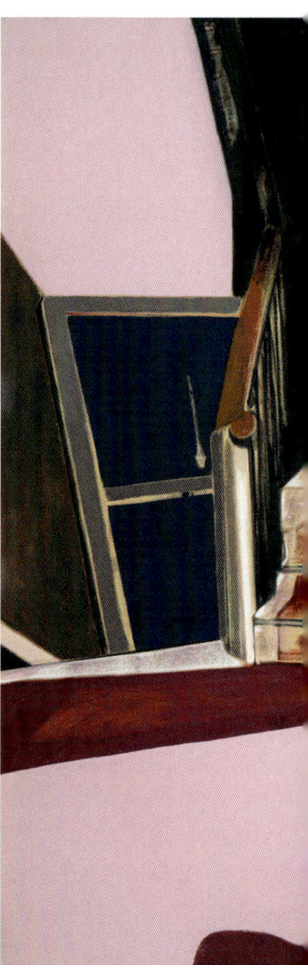

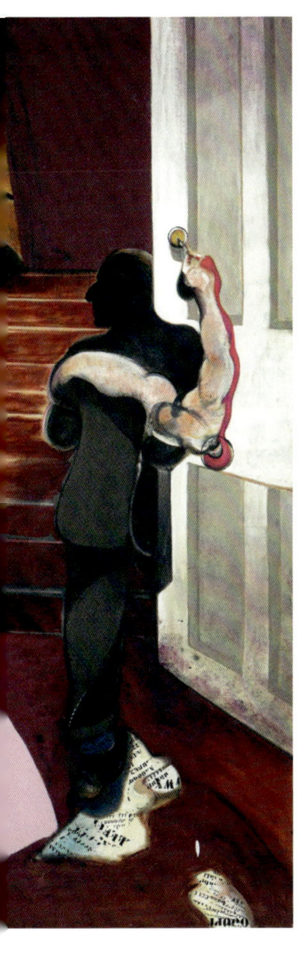

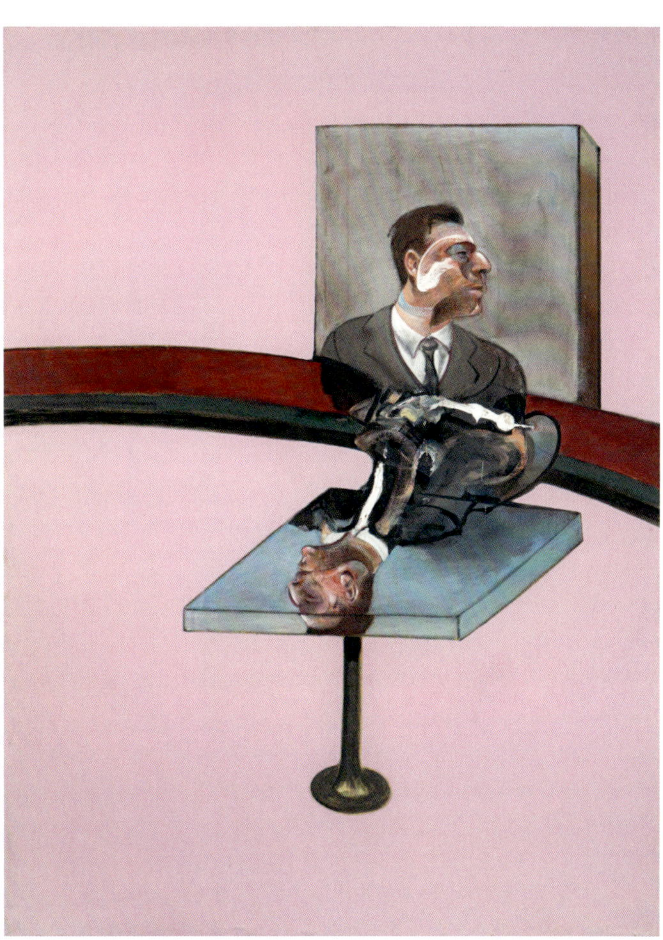

Louise Bourgeois (1911–2010)

In Respite, 1992

Steel, thread, and rubber, 328.9 × 81.2 × 71.1 cm

Louise Bourgeois's work *In Respite* consists of a metal post, over three meters in height, attached to which are spools of thread, like those found in a spinning factory. A hook is also fixed to the support, bearing an object in pink rubber with the shape of an elongated teardrop. Pinned to it is a small blue brooch from the artist's own jewelry collection. Sewing needles with black threads from the spools are also lodged in the pink rubber element. The title, *In Respite*, means "interval of rest or relief." Like many of this artist's works, the sculpture initially appears rational and even functional, but it also strikes a lyrical, poetic note, associated with the pink shape.

The work brings together a number of important elements from Bourgeois's expressive vocabulary. Spools and threads recall the spider, which, as both a notion and a motif, plays a significant role in her work: the spider, spinning threads to make yarn, is like a mother who can mend everything. The needles, which also occur in many of Bourgeois's works, are instruments of repair and healing. The artist is said to have regarded the black threads and the pinning of the needles into the rubber object as recurrent moments in the flow of time, interrupted by pauses for breath and opportunities for restoration and reconciliation. The hanging entity, which appears time and again in Bourgeois's work, in many variations and colors, could be a kind of surrogate for the unconscious: something that is present, but difficult to explain. The needle, as a means of repair, can be seen as supplying a connection between the unconscious and the conscious mind, thereby exemplifying the privileged access to the unconscious that, as Bourgeois repeatedly invoked, is enjoyed by the artist and denied to others.

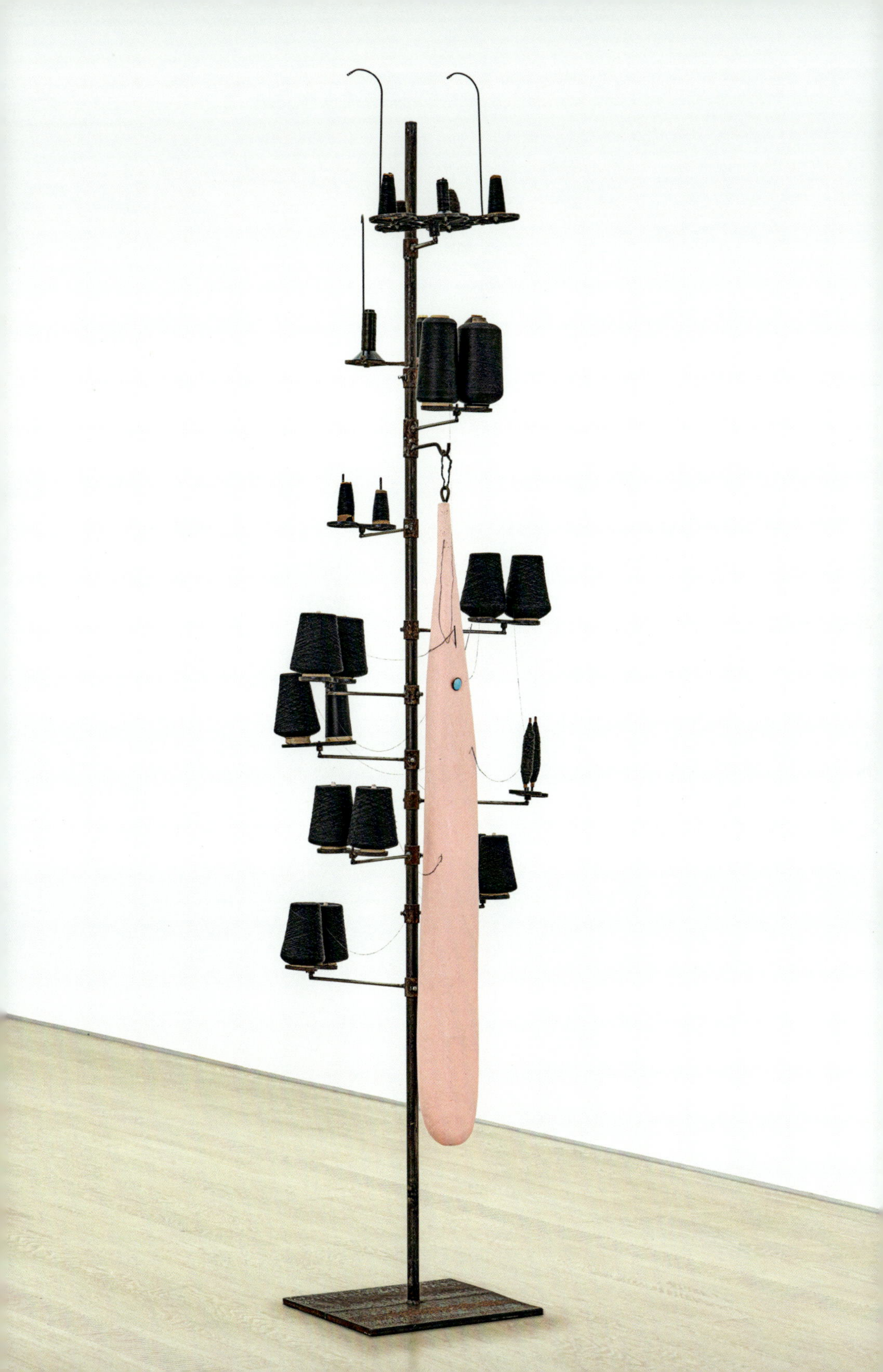

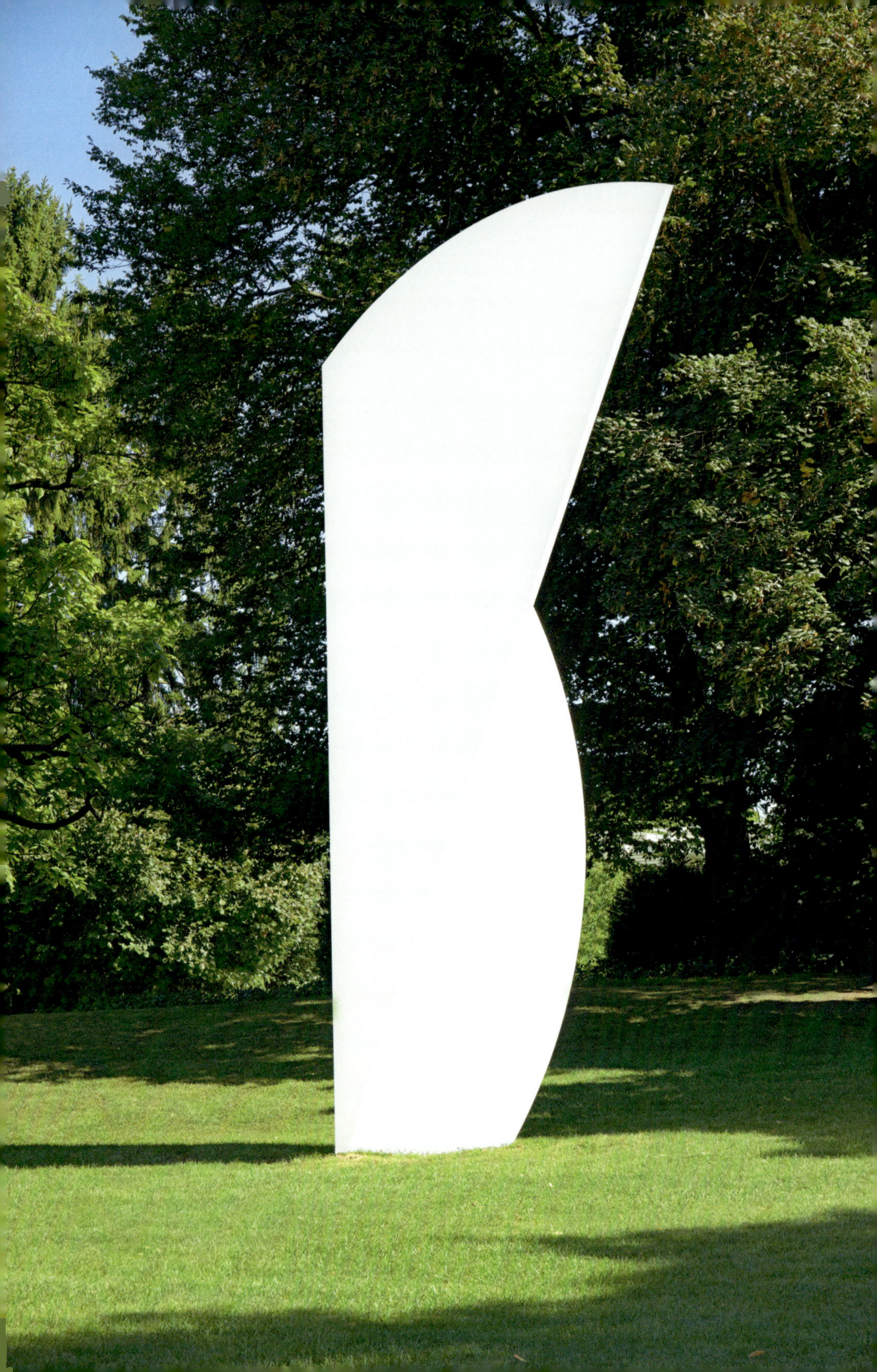

Ellsworth Kelly (1923–2015)

White Curves, 2001

Polyurethane paint on aluminum, 600 × 335 × 126 cm

Ellsworth Kelly's sculpture *White Curves*, a structure in gleaming white, rises up dynamically from the green surroundings of the Berower Park. It is cut from a simple basic shape, a segment of a circle, folded lengthwise.

The sculpture's form invites the viewer to look at it from several vantage points, each affording a particular experience of the work. Seen from a distance, the structure looks like a hand fan, tapering downward; but walking around it, the shape changes—into a spearhead, then an almond, and finally a sail inflated by the wind. The white-painted surface, flat and smooth as glass, picks up elements of light, shade, and the park landscape, and continually surprises the viewer with new reflections of the natural setting.

The idea for the six-meter-high sculpture emerged in connection with a series of works around the painting *Black Relief with White* (1994), which is also based on a segment of a circle and plays visually with the principle of folding. Yet it was Ernst Beyeler's visit to Kelly's studio in Spencertown, New York, in 1998, as part of the preparations for an exhibition devoted to the artist, that provided the decisive impulse for the further development of the work and the commission from the Fondation Beyeler.

From the 1950s onward, Kelly worked in parallel in the areas of painting and sculpture. He is known in particular for his so-called shaped canvases—paintings in a single color that are shaped in unusual ways. Working in the medium of sculpture was especially important in his quest for form. As Kelly himself put it: "I had to go through the sculpture stage, before I could . . . *shape* the canvas."

Today, the Beyeler Collection features seven works by Ellsworth Kelly. Besides various shaped canvases, which include *Blue Black Red Green* (2000) and *Lake II* (2002), *White Curves* is the only example of outdoor sculpture by the artist, and as such, inextricably linked with the Fondation Beyeler park.

Andy Warhol (1928–1987)

Flowers, 1965

Acrylic and silk-screen print on canvas,
213.4 × 369.3 cm

Andy Warhol was a protagonist of US-American Pop Art. His work is characterized by the use of motifs from advertising and the mass media. Following his early career as a commercial illustrator, he took up silk-screen printing and in 1960 began collecting motifs from flyers, newspapers, magazines, and movie programs; cutting them out; and using them for his screen prints.

The series of *Flowers*, at once concise and poetic, originated in the 1960s. Varying the flower motif with the silk-screen process, Warhol experimented with color combinations, various arrangements and numbers of flowers, and different print layers and formats. The image for the version of *Flowers* in the Beyeler Collection, dating from 1965, was taken from an American photography magazine. Warhol enlarged a section of the original and overexposed it to obscure the details of the hibiscus flower. In these works, the principle of seriality is applied with rigor.

For the *Flowers* in the Beyeler Collection, however, Warhol painted the blossoms and the green background by hand. The photographic reproduction of the individual flower became a simplified, infinitely repeatable decorative element in his series. The work of art no longer shows a facet of the natural world that can be appreciated in its individual beauty and depicted as unique. Instead, the plant undergoes a process of technical reproduction, beginning with the photograph and leading to the silk-screen print. Warhol transposed the fragility and impermanence of a delicate flower into a monumental dimension.

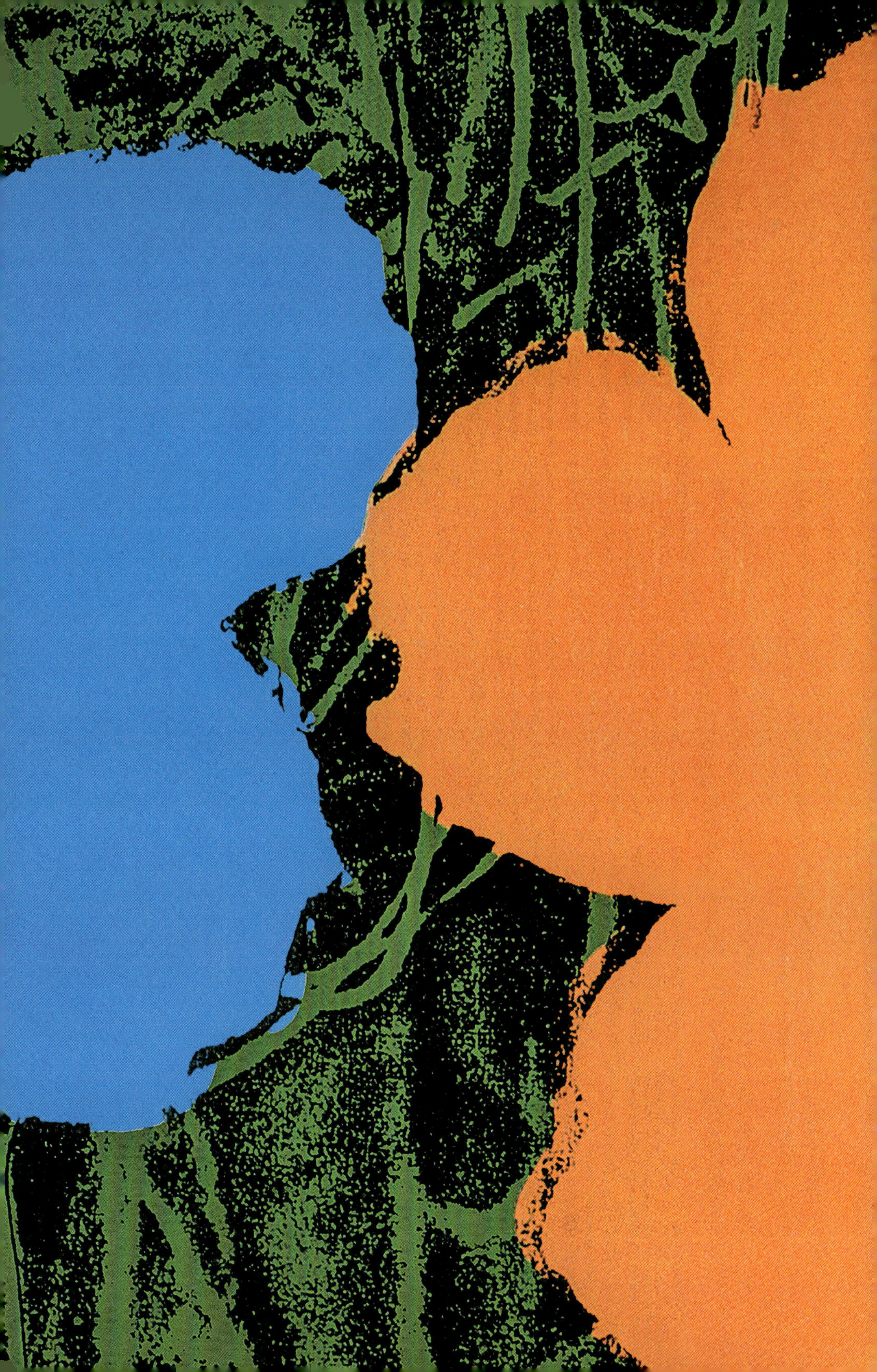

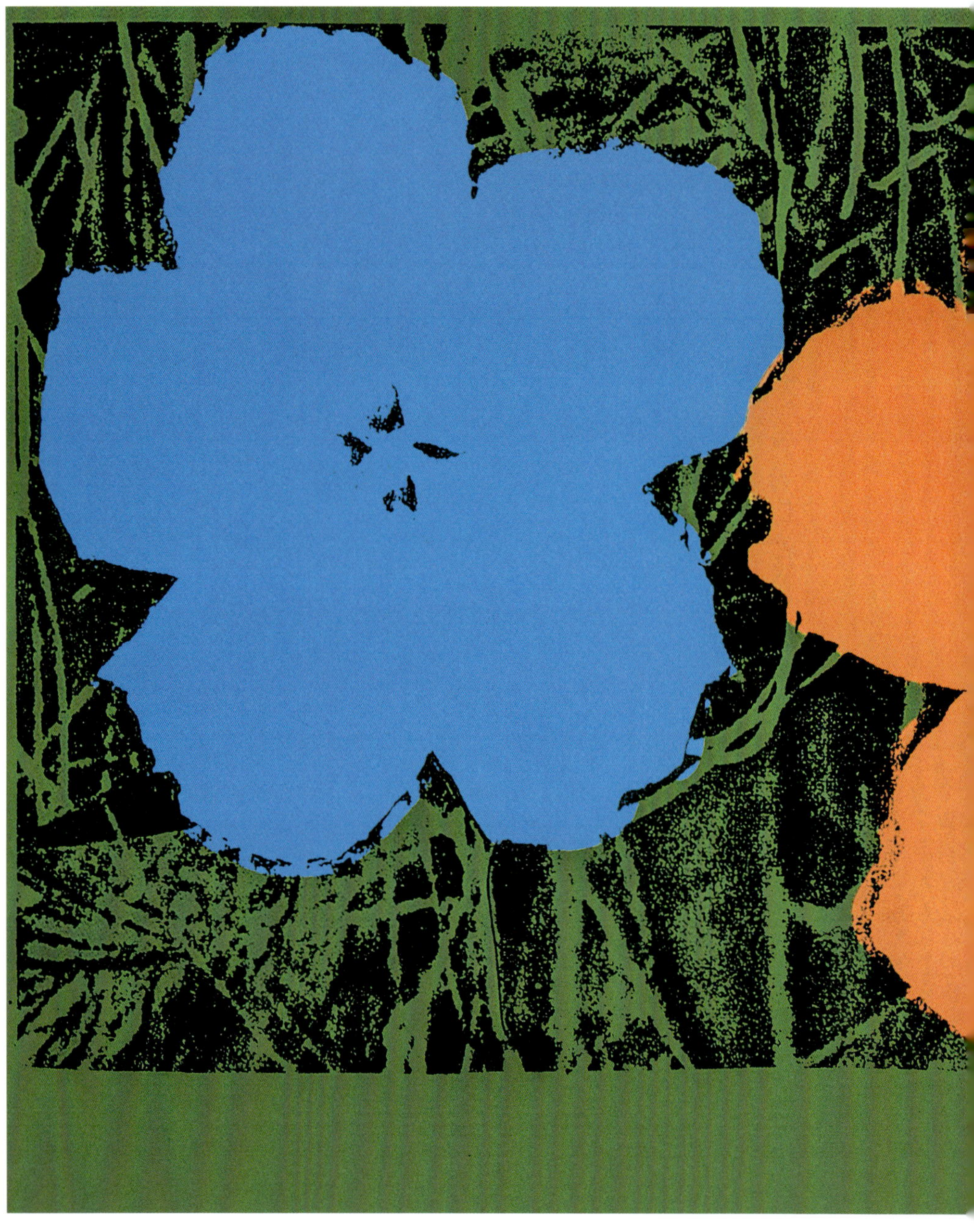

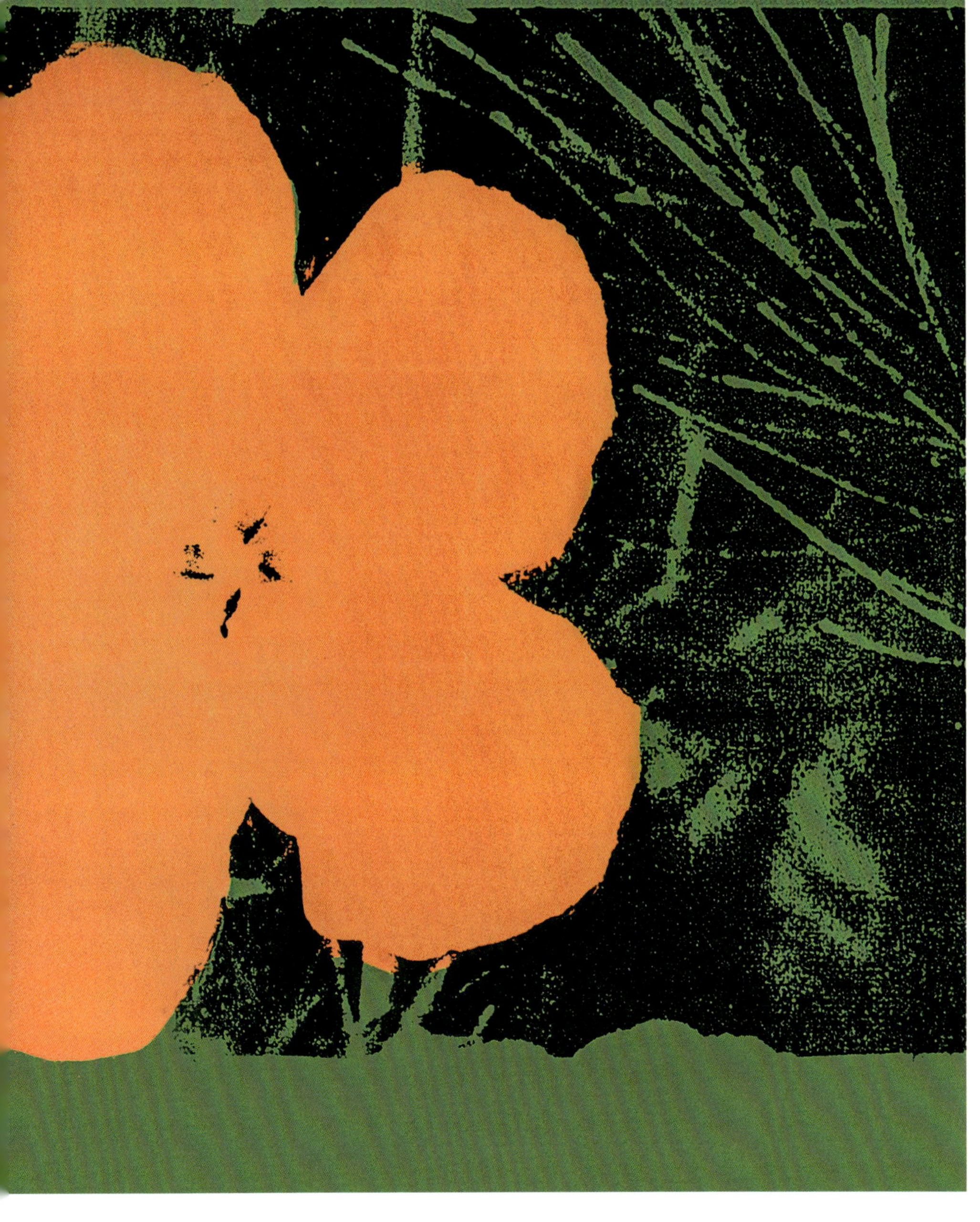

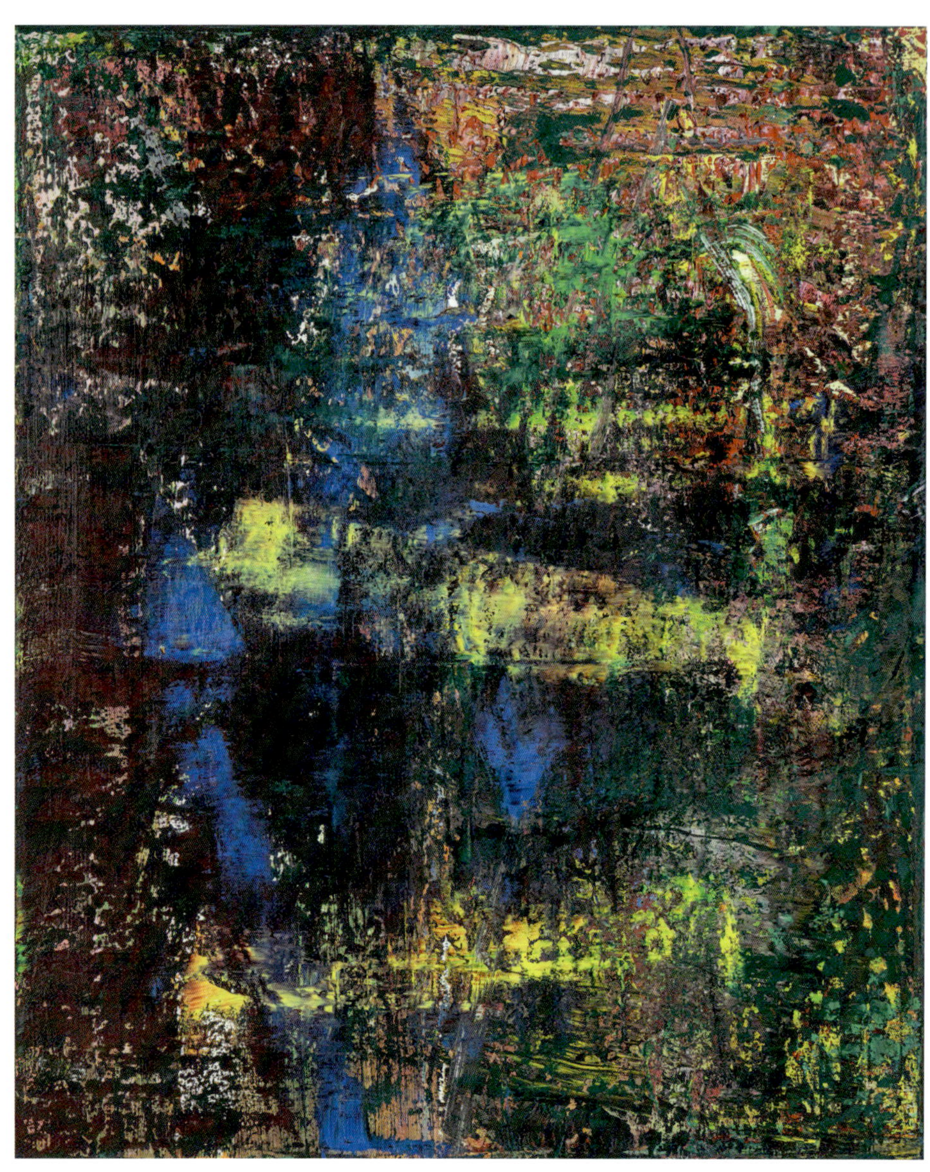

Gerhard Richter (b. 1932)

Lot | Lead, 1988

Oil on canvas, 300 × 250 cm

Gerhard Richter's oeuvre ranges from Photorealist portraits, landscapes, and still lifes, as well as abstract compositions, glass paintings, and digital prints, to works using mirrors and glass. His art is consistently fascinating in its alternation between figuration and abstraction, image and reproduction, control and chance, and its blurring of boundaries between painting, photography, digital printing, and sculpture.

Apart from individual pictures, Richter began creating numerous series, cycles, and spaces in the 1960s, to which the Fondation Beyeler devoted an exhibition in 2014. The starting point of this show was the large-scale work *Lot*, which, with *Schräge* (Slope), *Stand* (Position), and *Grad* (Degree) from the Museum Frieder Burda in Baden-Baden, belongs to a painting cycle made with a squeegee. Devised by Richter, the tool includes a long strip of Perspex and has been used by the artist since the early 1980s to apply, smudge, wipe and scrape off paint. The technique makes it possible to create multiple overlapping layers of paint, giving each work a unique structure. Parts of the surface can be scraped back to expose the colors beneath, and an interplay of sweeping movements in the act of painting becomes visible.

When using the squeegee, the outcome is only partly predictable. In an interview in 1999, Richter described the process as "a good technique for switching thought. I can't consciously calculate what will emerge. Subconsciously, though, I do have an inkling of it. It's a pleasant state of limbo." Working with chance has interested the artist for many years, at least since the early 1970s. In 1966 he made his first Color Chart pictures, inspired by commercial paint samples, with freely arranged squares or rectangles of color. Further Color Charts followed, from 1971 on, in which the arrangement of the colors was decided by a method of randomization specifically devised for the purpose. In later works, too, where color is poured or dripped onto the picture support, the application of the paint and the intermingling of colors follow a controlled principle of chance.

Marlene Dumas (b. 1953)

Broken White, 2006

Oil on canvas, 130 × 110 cm

The artist Marlene Dumas, born in South Africa and resident in Amsterdam since 1976, is chiefly concerned with the human figure and the portrait. Her paintings, drawings, and watercolors are at once contemporary and timeless, addressing themes that are central to human existence, such as love, sexuality, death, identity, and mourning.

Broken White shows a female figure with eyes closed in front of a red background. Her pale face, inclined sharply to one side, is framed by her black hair and the dark contour along her chin. With its narrow focus, the composition reveals a moment of detached calm and opens up numerous possibilities of interpretation. Is the figure asleep, exhausted, in a state of lust or pain, or perhaps even lifeless? As the title suggests, Dumas rejects the notion of purity that lies at the core of racist beliefs and therefore prefers off-white or other broken colors.

The painting is characterized by a striking play of contrasting colors. With the stark close-up view of the figure, the artist directs the viewer's full attention to the motif, facilitating an individual engagement with an emotional situation that is ambivalent and deeply human. The painting forms a kind of diptych with *The Swan* (2005), also in the collection of the Fondation Beyeler. The picture formats correspond, and the curving line of the chin and shoulder in *Broken White* is echoed in the wing of the white swan.

Dumas's approach to her painting and subject matter is complex and nuanced. She never paints directly from life but finds inspiration for her work in photographs stored in a personal archive of source materials, including magazines, newspapers, art exhibition catalogues, and films. *Broken White*, too, is based on a photograph: a detail, greatly enlarged, from a black-and-white image by the Japanese photographer Nobuyoshi Araki. Through her painterly gesture, Dumas transforms the original into a fascinating picture that is poignant and somewhat disturbing.

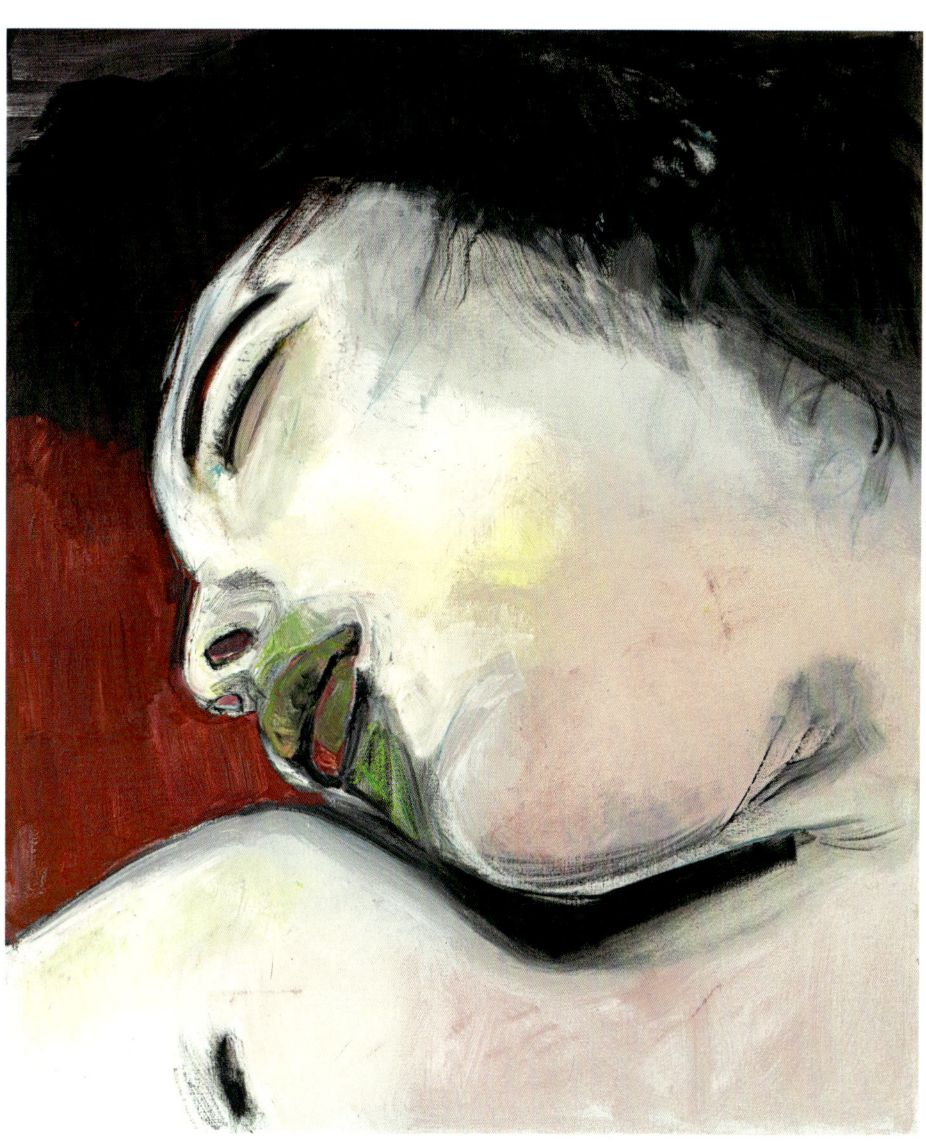

Thomas Schütte (b. 1954)

Hase | Hare, 2013

Patinated bronze, height ca. 400 cm

The sculptor Thomas Schütte was born in Oldenburg in 1954. Since the early 1980s he has been preoccupied with the human figure in its various forms of expression. His work is characterized by a playful and unconventional approach to form, material, color, and light.
His bronze sculpture *Hase*, a monumental fountain standing in the center of the lily pond in the Fondation Beyeler park, is supplemented in the collection by a substantial group of other works, including powerfully expressive figures and delicate watercolor portraits. The central point of connection between Schütte's oeuvre and the work of other artists in the collection is the exploration of the image of the human subject in modern art.
From 1973 to 1981, at a time when the Rhineland was a center of the international art world, Schütte studied at the Academy of Fine Arts Düsseldorf under Fritz Schwegler and Gerhard Richter. His work continues to display a fine gift of observation, casting an ironic eye on things that dominate everyday life, coupled with a radical eagerness to experiment.
The toy-like bronze hare, based on a modeling-clay figure made by Schütte's daughter, is at once demonic and comically grotesque as it gazes at the viewer from the lily pond with an expression that combines mischief with gravity. Its pose is unnaturally distorted, lending it a semi-human appearance that, with its flaws and lifelike traits, has an unsettling effect. The material contrast between bronze and modeling clay as well as the ambivalence between monstrosity and childish fantasy are omnipresent.

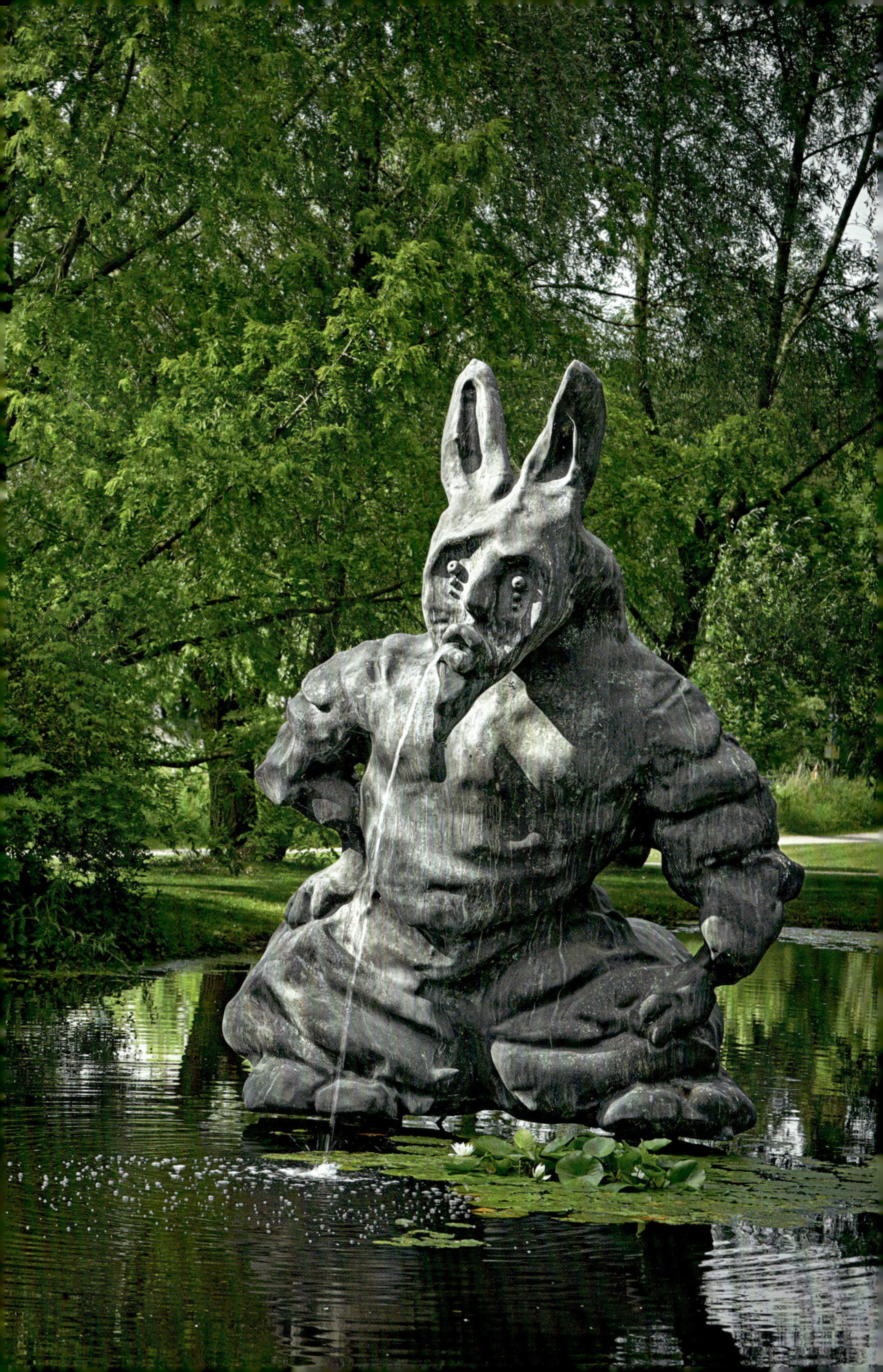

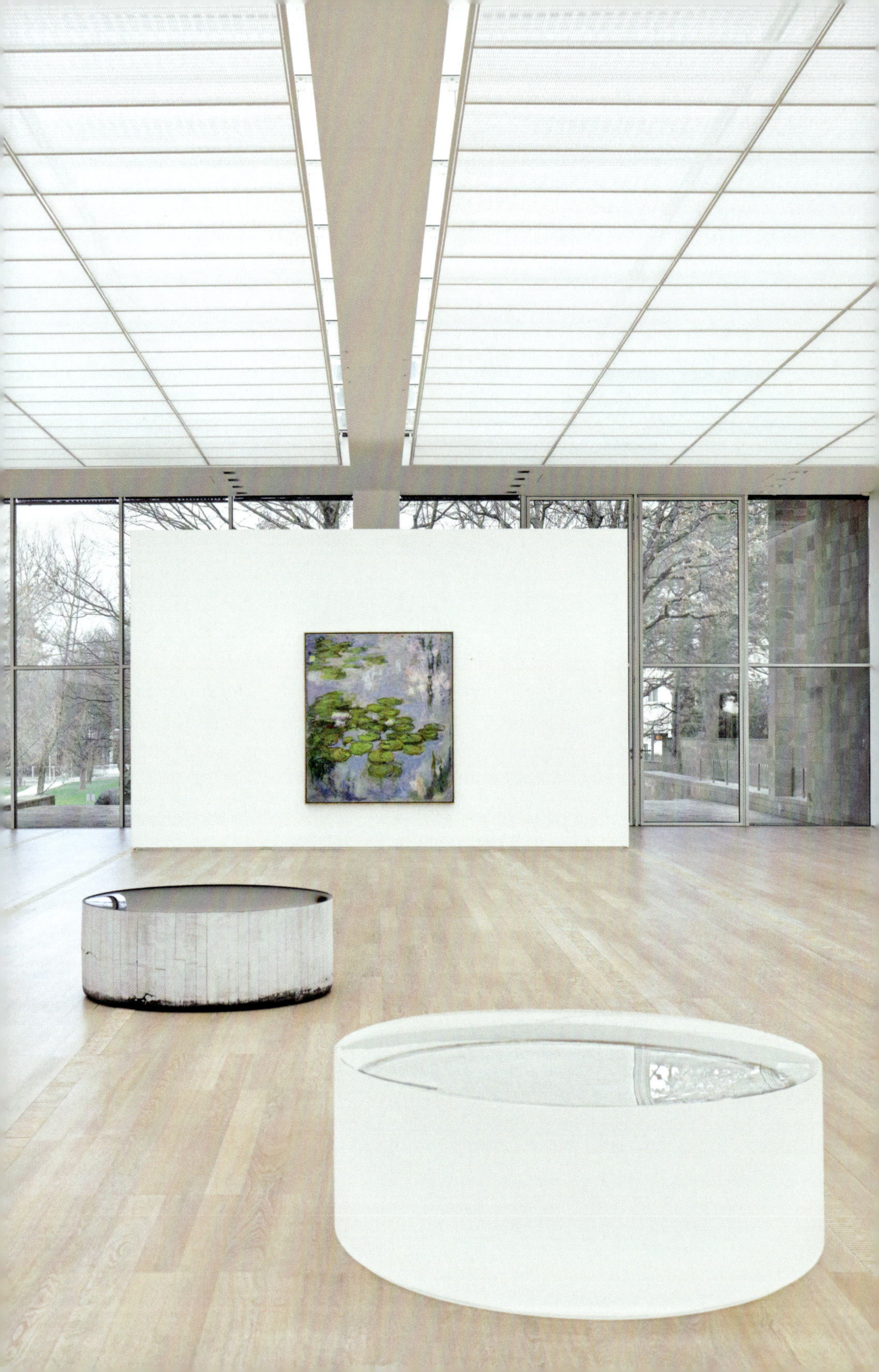

Roni Horn (b. 1955)

Opposites of White, 2006–07
Solid cast glass with as-cast surfaces,
2 units, height 51 cm, diameter 143 cm each

The focus of Roni Horn's art is on the plurality and changeability of people, places, and things. Through her drawings, photographic installations, sculptures, books, and texts, the American artist gives shape to ambivalences and transformations, enabling the viewer to experience them in sensual terms.

Since the mid-1990s, Horn has been making monumental sculptures in glass—an amorphous material that, in terms of chemistry or physics, is neither liquid nor solid, but instead exists somewhere between the two states of matter. The two-unit sculpture *Opposites of White* in the collection of the Fondation Beyeler illustrates these two ambivalent and impalpable properties of the artist's material. The rough sides of the two glass forms, weighing around two tons each, are marked by the casting process, with traces that are more or less evident, depending on the surface structure of the mold. In contrast, the circular tops appear transparent and flawless.

These clear, gleaming circles invite the viewer to gaze into the interior of the glass sculptures. The surface, like a pool of water on a clear, windless day, shows reflections and visual effects that vary with the lighting conditions, the weather, the time of day, and the surroundings. While the simple form of the two sculptures has associations with Minimal Art, the impression of minimalist objectivity and clarity is dispelled in the act of perception. The fluctuating appearance of Horn's poetic works ultimately eludes definition and repeatedly defies the gaze in its search for specificity. It remains uncertain whether the sculptures are solid or liquid, light or dark, buoyant or heavy.

Wolfgang Tillmans (b. 1968)

Anders (Brighton Arcimboldo), 2005

C-print on Forex in artist's frame, 204 × 135 cm

Anders (Brighton Arcimboldo) is a framed black-and-white photograph, over two meters tall. The title, as so often with Wolfgang Tillmans, is a simple enumeration of facts: the name of the person portrayed, the place where the photograph was taken, and an art-historical reference. What we see is a young man in left profile whose head and face are partly covered with pebbles. The image is uncanny, perhaps disturbing, and yet deeply fascinating. This is a photograph full of contrasts that imbue the image with tension, life, and vibrancy. Large, heavy pebbles are laid on the delicate skin of the cheek, nose, and temple. The luminous white of the man's T-shirt stands out sharply from the dark background. The flatness of the white and black areas contrasts with the marked three-dimensionality of the rounded stones. The subject's relaxed, peaceful expression corresponds unexpectedly to the cool appearance of the pebbles, resting lightly on his face.

Giuseppe Arcimboldo was a sixteenth-century Italian painter famed for his portraits composed of flowers and fruits or inanimate objects. In his portrait, Tillmans takes the opposite approach: instead of obscuring the face with the pebbles, he emphasizes its fragility through the photographic contrasts.

Anders (Brighton Arcimboldo) is a characteristic example of Tillmans's original and boldly expressive visual language, which sharpens the gaze and brings elements to light that are otherwise overlooked. The work belongs to a substantial group of photographs by the artist in the collection of the Fondation Beyeler. It can be exhibited separately or as part of an ensemble devised by Tillmans for a wall or an entire room. The visual dialogues thereby generated between individual pictures continually open up new perspectives on what initially may seem familiar.

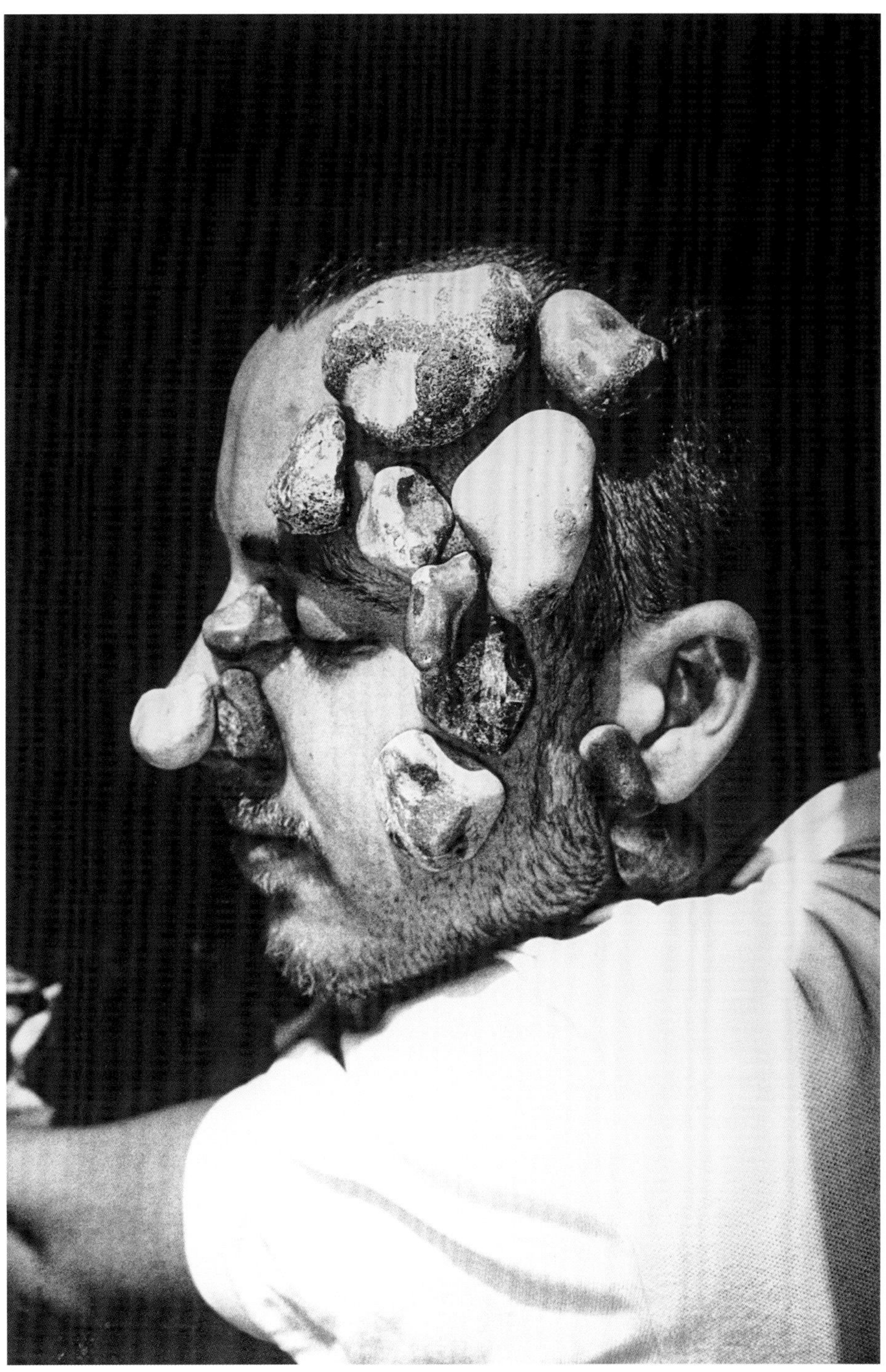

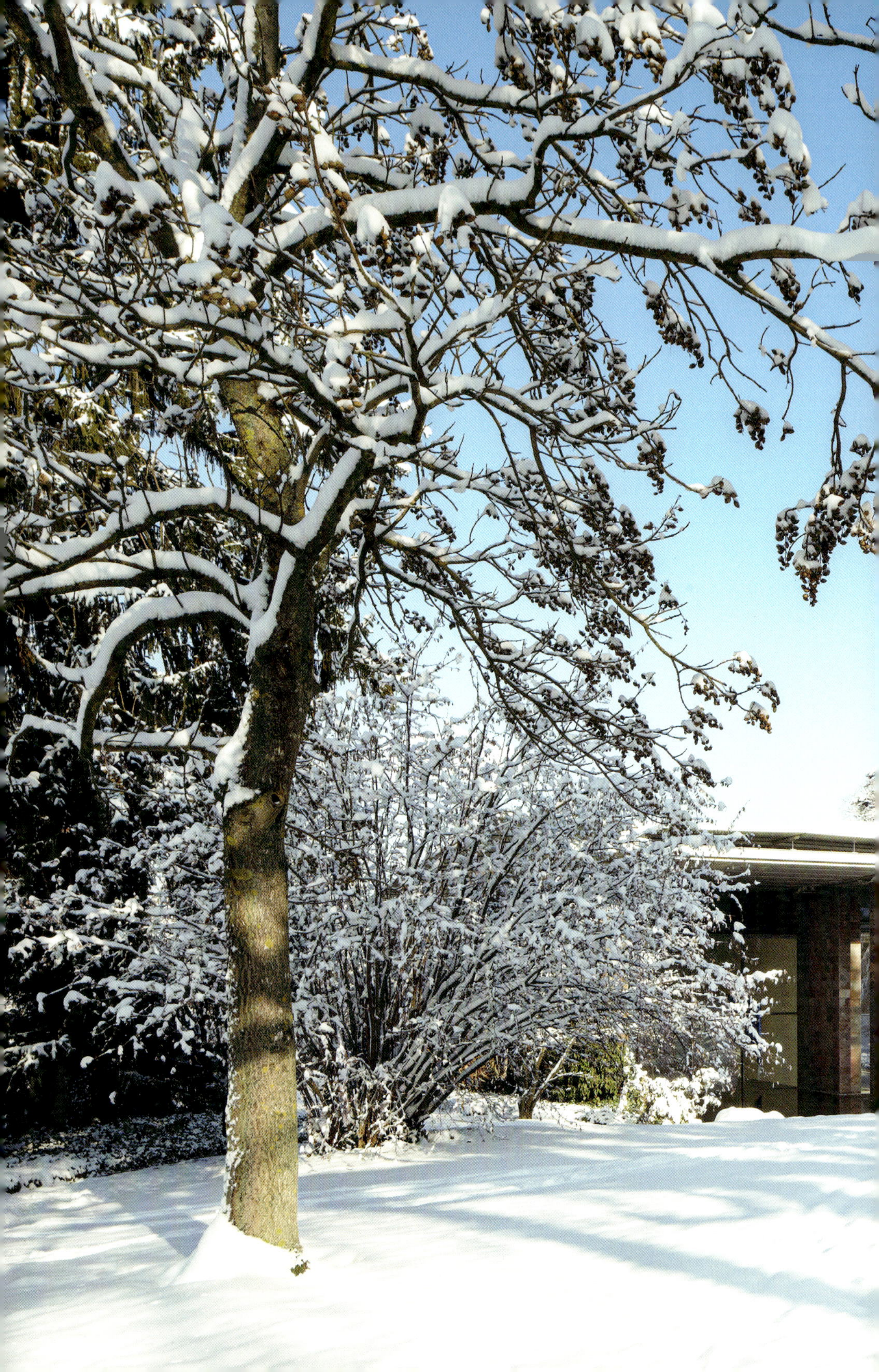

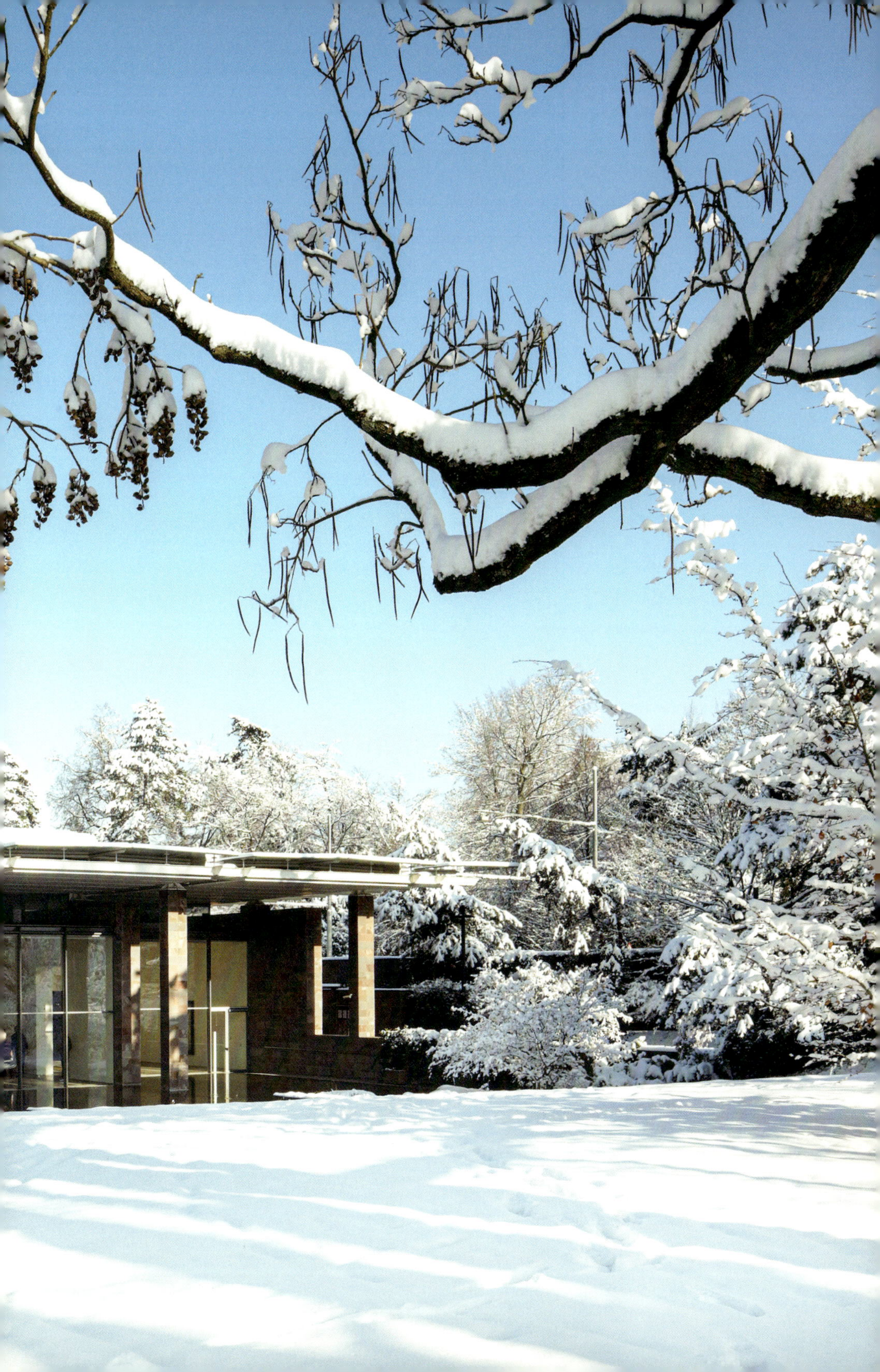

Published by

Fondation Beyeler

Authors

Amelie Baader: 1, 4, 8
Raphaël Bouvier: Introduction, 6, 10, 11
Stefanie Bringezu: 3, 9
Christine Burger: 14
Marlene Bürgi: 22, 24
Sylvie Felber: 17
Victoria Gellner: 16
Fiona Hesse: 5
Michiko Kono: 21
Ulf Küster: 2, 15, 18
Charlotte Sarrazin: 7, 20, 23
Janine Schmutz: 19
Rahel Schrohe: 13
Magdalena Syen: 12
Theodora Vischer: 25

Concept

Raphaël Bouvier, Fondation Beyeler

Editing

Romina Del Principe and Franziska Stegmann, Fondation Beyeler

Copyediting

Joann Skrypzak-Davidsmeyer, Cologne

Translation

John Ormrod, Munich

Graphic design

Silke Fahnert, Uwe Koch, Cologne

Production

Christine Stäcker, Stuttgart

Reproductions

Repromayer Medienproduktion GmbH, Reutlingen

Printing

Offizin Scheufele, Stuttgart

Binding

Idupa Schübelin GmbH, Owen

A publication of the
Fondation Beyeler

Baselstrasse 101
4125 Riehen/Basel
Switzerland
Tel. +41 61 6459-700
www.fondationbeyeler.ch
info@fondationbeyeler.ch

Hatje Cantz Verlag GmbH

Mommsenstrasse 27
10629 Berlin
Germany
www.hatjecantz.de
A Ganske Publishing Group company

ISBN 978-3-7757-5396-8 (English)
ISBN 978-3-7757-5781-2 (French)
ISBN 978-3-7757-5395-1 (German)

Printed in Germany

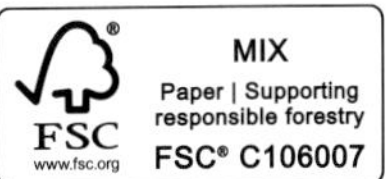

Cover illustration

Claude Monet, *Le bassin aux nymphéas*, ca. 1917–20 (detail)

Frontispiece

Exterior view with Claude Monet's *Le bassin aux nymphéas*, ca. 1917–20, and Alberto Giacometti's *L'homme qui marche II*, 1960

Following pages

South façade of the Fondation Beyeler building, designed by Renzo Piano

Berower Park with Alexander Calder's *The Tree*, 1966, and Ellsworth Kelly's *White Curves*, 2001

Photo credits

Friedel Ammann, Basel: autumn scene

Robert Bayer, Basel: 2, 3, 6–10, 12, 13, 15–23, 25, Giacometti exhibition view

Thomas Koenig, Stuttgart: frontispiece

Mark Niedermann, Riehen/Basel: 24; Matisse exhibition view; spring scene, summer scene, winter scene

Peter Schibli, Basel: 1, 4, 5, 11, 14

Text sources

3: English translation of the full title of Rousseau's painting by John Ormrod.

4: Vincent van Gogh, letter to his mother and sister, ca. July 11, 1890, https://vangoghletters.org/vg/letters/let899/letter.html (accessed January 30, 2024).

5: Ernst Beyeler, in *Das Auge des Sammlers: Ernst Beyeler und seine Schätze: Ein Film zu den Werken der Sammlung Beyeler*, directed and written by Edith Jud, produced by Fondation Beyeler/3Sat, DVD, first released on VHS: Basileafilm AG 2007 [1997], 58 min., 10'38" min.; and Wassily Kandinsky, letter to Gabriele Münter, January 31, 1904, cit. in Jelena Hahl-Koch, *Kandinsky* (London, 1993), pp. 93–94.

6: Henri Matisse, "Jazz," in *Matisse on Art*, ed. Jack Flam (Berkeley and Los Angeles, 1995), pp. 171–74, here p. 172.

8: Constantin Brancusi, cit. in Carola Giedion-Welcker, *Constantin Brancusi* (New York, 1959), p. 198.

19: Ellsworth Kelly, cit. in *Neuzugänge 1998–2003 / Recent Acquisitions 1998–2003*, Fondation Beyeler (Riehen/Basel, 2003), p. 50.

21: Gerhard Richter, "Interview with Stefan Koldehoff, 1999," in *Gerhard Richter: Text: Writings, Interviews and Letters 1961–2007*, ed. Dietmar Elger and Hans Ulrich Obrist (London, 2009), p. 353.

Josef Albers Pawel Althamer Francis Alÿs Harold Ancart Leonor Antunes Michael Armitage Hans Arp Lucas Arruda Francis Bacon Georg Baselitz Jean-Michel Basquiat Pierre Bonnard Louise Bourgeois Constantin Brancusi Georges Braque Alexander Calder Paul Cézanne Marc Chagall Eduardo Chillida Christo & Jeanne-Claude Enrico David Tacita Dean Edgar Degas Peter Doig Jean Dubuffet Marlene Dumas Olafur Eliasson Max Ernst Jean Fautrier Fischli/Weiss Lucio Fontana Günther Förg Sam Francis Alberto Giacometti Felix Gonzalez-Torres Wade Guyton Duane Hanson Jenny Holzer Roni Horn Pierre Huyghe Sergej Jensen Wassily Kandinsky Ellsworth Kelly Anselm Kiefer Paul Klee Fernand Léger Roy Lichtenstein Jacques Lipchitz Kazimir Malevich Henri Matisse Joan Miró Piet Mondrian Claude Monet Sarah Morris Ernesto Neto Barnett Newman Otobong Nkanga Philippe Parreno Elizabeth Peyton Susan Philipsz Pablo Picasso Sigmar Polke Jackson Pollock Neo Rauch Robert Rauschenberg Ad Reinhardt Gerhard Richter Auguste Rodin Mark Rothko Henri Rousseau Doris Salcedo Wilhelm Sasnal Thomas Schütte Tino Sehgal Richard Serra Georges Seurat Frank Stella Rudolf Stingel Antoni Tàpies Wayne Thiebaud Wolfgang Tillmans Jean Tinguely Rirkrit Tiravanija Mark Tobey Vincent van Gogh Andy Warhol Franz West Rachel Whiteread Jordan Wolfson